The Development
of
Political Theory
and
Government

By
Mortimer J. Adler
and
Peter Wolff

Preface by
The Honorable William Benton

1959

ENCYCLOPÆDIA BRITANNICA, INC.

Chicago

PREFACE

This Reading Plan deals with the problems of government and politics. It guides the reader through a discussion of these problems by some of the great writers of the past. The writings range all the way from the Book of Samuel to John Stuart Mill's work on liberty. The problems vary from the establishment of the Israelite monarchy 3,000 years ago to the establishment of liberal government in 19th-century England, from Plato's quest for an ideal commonwealth to the brilliant analyses by Hamilton and Madison of how freedom can be safeguarded in a stable, effective government.

Perhaps you pride yourself on your practical bent of mind. What help, you may ask, can such visionaries as Samuel, Plato, and Aristotle offer us moderns in our daily tasks of government? What do these ancients have to do with our problems or we with theirs?

Please remember a penetrating observation made by Lord Keynes: "The ideas of economists and political philosophers, both when they are right and when they are wrong, are more powerful than is commonly understood. Indeed, the world is ruled by little else. Practical men, who believe themselves to be quite exempt from any intellectual influences, are usually the slaves of some defunct economist. Madmen in authority, who hear voices in the air, are distilling their frenzy from some academic scribbler of a few years back."

And among Western peoples it is we Americans—the people whose "call to greatness" was never clearer—who have in recent decades been most indifferent to political and social philosophy, including our own.

I have been active in business and government most of my life. I have had the opportunity and privilege of serving my country in the U. S. Senate, the State Department, and the United Nations. Nothing is more obvious to me than the fact that our continued existence as civilized men rests on the art of politics.

Politics is the most vital of the human arts. It is an art that has to be learned. And it is a difficult art. Einstein said, "Politics is more difficult than physics." You will certainly agree with Einstein that our world is more likely to die of bad politics than of bad physics.

Oversimplifying: there are two kinds of innocents in practical affairs. The first kind wants to rely on experience alone— usually the experience he himself has had. The second kind wants to get by on theory alone, possibly pure and undefiled by contact with everyday experience.

The best way to attain sound political judgment is surely through a combination of practical experience and liberal learning. That is what is so heartening about this Reading Plan. Through it we may converse with men who were both wise and experienced. If we rely wholly on homespun political pragmatism, pragmatism will too often fail to meet its own test—that is, it won't work! We must add to it the observations of the great thinkers and writers about politics.

Make no mistake about the practical experience of these "thinkers" or "visionaries." Plato's early interests were political. In later life he tried to train a king for right rule. Aristotle was the tutor of Alexander the Great. He probably wrote some of his political treatises for the edification of that world conqueror. Tacitus was a senator. Machiavelli was a career official in the diplomatic service of the Republic of Florence. Jefferson, Hamilton, Madison, and Jay were active revolutionists and statesmen. None of these writers was a lodger in an ivory tower.

The authors of these readings faced essentially the same kinds of political questions we face today: what are the ends of political life? What is the best form of government to serve these ends? What is the proper relation between government and the individual, between government and religion?

This Reading Plan permits us to listen to the answers given by the great writers of our Western tradition to the basic questions about how men can best live together in political society. The Plan offers no single answer or no single view. If it confuses you to hear more than one voice, stop right here. Our "greats" often disagree with one another. At the end you will still have to decide for yourself. In this, this Reading Plan accords with the democratic way which places high value on the right to differ and dissent—even from the powers that be. It also accords with the way of liberal education which places its faith in the free intelligence of the individual human being and tries to develop the intellectual virtues which justify that faith.

You will find continuity and concentration throughout these readings as well as difference and dispersion. Aristotle tells us that "man is a political animal." He shows that man alone among living beings has a sense of good and evil, of justice and injustice. "Justice," he says, "is the principle of order in human society." Echoing Aristotle more than 2,000 years later, our own countryman, James Madison, in *The Federalist*, No. 51, reflected: "Justice is the end of government. It is the end of civil society. It ever has been and ever will be pursued until it be obtained, or until liberty be lost in the pursuit."

Someone has said that a nation won't acquire wisdom except through the love of it. And the love of wisdom calls for a certain amount of determination.

To set oneself the task of acquiring some mastery of the Western political heritage is an act of dedication. No reading guide, no lecture series, no commentaries can make this an easy task. But if you carry the task through it will enrich your own life and the life of your community and your country, too.

I have found that the personal satisfactions that come to a public servant (along with hard knocks!) have no parallels in private life. Public service calls forth one's highest capabilities. It challenges every man to work toward that goal which has been defined as the essence of happiness: activity that develops his highest power. Whatever the degree of his involvement in politics, every man who becomes a concerned and active citizen can share in such rewards.

I wish you good learning in the use of this Plan. But I wish you more than that. I wish you the kind of learning that bears fruit in your actual life as a citizen—in your precinct, in your town and county and state, and in the family of nations.

Good reading and good politics! I know of no better wish for most of us.

William Benton

FOREWORD

This Reading Plan deals with problems in one field: government and political theory. You need not have done the readings in the Introductory Plan to undertake these readings. However, we make occasional references to the introductory readings for those readers who have already done them. For example, in the first assignment, Plato, *Republic*, Books II-IV, we refer back to the second assignment in the first Reading Plan, *Republic*, Books I and II, and to the guide to that assignment. We make similar references in the second, eleventh, and thirteenth readings in this series. These are merely suggestions and aids to further study.

How to Use the Reading Plan. This guide contains three parts: (1) a list of readings; (2) guides to each of the readings; and (3) suggestions for additional readings.

1. *The Reading List.* There are fifteen readings. You should take about two weeks for each reading. The length of each reading is designed for that period.

2. *The Guides.* These should prove most helpful to the reader of the *Great Books* who is going it alone, without teacher, discussion leader, or other study aids. The purpose of the guide is to help you to get started on an assignment by providing you with background material and by stimulating your thinking about the reading. The background material may consist of information about the author's life and work, or

about the historical circumstances under which the book was written. Or it may remark on the form and style of the book being studied; it may discuss, for example, the dialogue as a form for presenting philosophic ideas, or observe the difference between historical and poetic writing.

A large portion of each guide deals with what the reading says. The high lights are pointed out, often by quotation. Difficult passages are discussed and explained. The structure of the whole book is considered, and the individual parts are related to it. Above all, attention is called to the relevance of the book to present-day situations and issues. Examples and questions help to show how the book is related to our thinking today.

Special problems are presented for you, the critical reader, to think about. These problems are not mere questions that can be answered by repeating what the text says. The statement of a problem is followed by a brief discussion which illuminates the problem, indicates some of the possible answers, and emphasizes the importance of the question. Some readers will be satisfied simply to read the problems, and to give them some thought. Others may want to write out answers to them. The questions cannot be answered by a mere "yes" or "no," or "true" or "false." Each problem requires real analysis, and several paragraphs or even an essay may be needed for the answer. Since there is no "right" answer to these questions, and since their main purpose is to stimulate some thought about the reading matter, you alone will be able to check and judge your answer.

Each guide concludes with a section entitled QUESTIONS. This section gives you an opportunity to check the thoroughness of your reading. In this section, there are a series of questions—anywhere from half a dozen to a dozen—about the reading. They are factual questions and can therefore be answered in a definite fashion. The information asked for is in the reading. A list of the pages where the answers may be found appears at the end of Part II of the Reading Plan, pages 219-221. You can check your accuracy by referring to that list.

3. *Additional Readings.* These give you an opportunity to delve more deeply into the subject of politics. We have tried to provide considerable variety. Here you will find other books on politics and government, including some by the authors in the reading list, as well as books about the authors, and books that provide historical and social background for some of the problems raised. We have tried to suggest two types of works: (1) books that are as good or almost as good as those in the Reading Plan; and (2) contemporary books that give you some notion of the important current problems in political theory and how they are being treated. Since most of these works themselves suggest a wealth of bibliographical material, there is almost no end to the amount of suggested reading that is presented to you here.

There is considerably more unity in this Reading Plan than in the *General Introduction to the Great Books.* Nevertheless, the readings also contain considerable variety, for the subject of politics has many aspects. You may find it useful to get a preliminary glimpse of the various topics and lines of thought that run throughout these fifteen readings. In the guides to the readings we have concentrated largely on four topics:

1. *The nature and origin of the state.* Here we must face the question of whether there was an actual historical moment when the state first came to be, and also the question of the condition in which men lived (either really or hypothetically) before there was any state. Does man before he becomes a member of a state live in a "state of nature"? Or is it correct to say that civil society is man's natural state or condition? What, finally, is the precise manner in which men form a state?

These and related questions are discussed in Plato's *Republic,* Aristotle's *Politics,* Hobbes's *Leviathan,* and Rousseau's *Social Contract.* Of course these readings also touch on many other topics; and it should be remembered that questions concerning the origin and nature of the state are also raised in many of the other readings.

2. *The forms of government.* The main questions here concern the best form of government. There are two chief candidates for the honor: aristocracy and democracy. The supporters

of each of these forms of government usually base their reasoning on divergent views of human nature. The advocates of aristocracy maintain that only a few—the highly gifted and highly educated—are fit to govern. The proponents of democracy maintain that all men have a right to participate in government as citizens with suffrage. These matters are discussed by Plato and Aristotle, by Hobbes, Montesquieu, and Rousseau, by Kant and Mill.

3. *Popular forms of government.* Thinkers who agree that the people are the ultimate source of all political power, and that they should retain a leverage of power against government disagree as to whether the popular will should be expressed directly or through representatives. Some think that popular government means direct, pure democracy. Others maintain that the people can delegate their powers to representatives without losing their essential role. This point is argued by Locke, Montesquieu, Rousseau, Kant, and Mill.

4. *Law and lawmaking.* What distinguishes civil society from a state of anarchy is man-made law. Historians recognize that disrespect for law, or bad laws, are among the causes for the downfall of states. So we find much concern for laws in the writings of Plutarch, Tacitus, and Shakespeare, as well as in formal political writings, such as Aquinas' *Treatise on Law*, Montesquieu's *Spirit of Laws*, Kant's *Science of Right*, and Hegel's *Philosophy of Right*.

Many other topics, besides these four, are touched upon in these fifteen readings. You will discover these for yourself as you proceed. But it will be helpful if you keep at least these four topics in mind as you read, and try to discover what each reading has to say about them.

CONTENTS

A NOTE ON

REFERENCE STYLE

In referring to *Great Books of the Western World,* the same style is used as in the *Syntopicon.* Pages are cited by number and section. In books that are printed in single column, "a" and "b" refer to the upper and lower half of the page. In books that are printed in double column, "a" and "b" refer to the upper and lower half of the left column, "c" and "d" to the upper and lower half of the right column. For example, "Vol. 53, p. 210b" refers to the lower half of page 210, since Vol. 53, James's *Principles of Psychology,* is printed in single column. But "Vol. 7, p. 202b" refers to the lower left quarter of page 202, since Vol. 7, Plato's *Dialogues,* is printed in double column.

In Bible references, if there is a difference between the King James and the Douay version, the King James reference is given first, followed by (D) and the Douay reference.

THE READING LIST

1 PLATO, *The Republic*, Books II-V. Vol. 7, pp. 310-373. (Also, *The Republic*, Books I-II. Vol. 7, pp. 295-324.)

2 ARISTOTLE, *Politics*, Books III-IV. Vol. 9, pp. 471-502. (Also, *Politics*, Book I. Vol. 9, pp. 445-455.)

3 PLUTARCH, *The Lives of the Noble Grecians and Romans.* "Agis," "Cleomenes," "Tiberius Gracchus," "Caius Gracchus," "Caius and Tiberius Gracchus and Agis and Cleomenes Compared." Vol. 14, pp. 648-691.

4 OLD TESTAMENT, I Samuel, (D) I Kings. NEW TESTAMENT, Matthew, 22:15-22; Acts, 21:1-26: 32.

5 TACITUS, *The Annals*, Books I, XIII-XVI. Vol. 15, pp. 1-23, 125-184.

6 AQUINAS, *Summa Theologica*, Part I-II, QQ. 90-97. Vol. 20, pp. 205-239.

7 MACHIAVELLI, *The Prince*. Vol. 23, pp. 1-37.

8 HOBBES, *Leviathan*. Introduction and Ch. 13-21. Vol. 23, pp. 47, 84-117.

9 SHAKESPEARE, *King Henry the Fourth*, Parts I and II. Vol. 26, pp. 434-502.

PLATO

The Republic

Books II–V

Vol. 7, pp. 310–373

Also, PLATO

The Republic

Books I–II

Vol. 7, pp. 295–324

For a discussion of this assignment,
see the Second Reading in

A General Introduction to the Great Books

Plato's blueprint for an ideal community has been the subject of inspiration and execration for almost 2,500 years. This writing has shocked some people by its proposal of equality for women and the possession of all things in common, including wives and children. It has shocked others by its portrayal of an authoritarian, hierarchical state, with a "guardian" elite, a philosopher-king, and a "royal lie" to keep the lower classes content. Plato's "republic" has been called Fascist, Communist, totalitarian. It has also been considered a heavenly city and has inspired many similar works in the Western tradition. And its influence has come down the centuries to utopian communities in the United States, such as New Harmony, Indiana, and Oneida, New York, and to the communal settlements in modern Israel.

Plato himself tells us that he has set before us an ideal state—"a city in the skies"—to serve as a measure of the quality of the actual states we live in. He put us at a distance from the everyday scene and frees us from the lock step of daily routine, so that we may come into contact with essential truths. He directs us to what man can be and should do. The picture he gives us of an ideal community provides a vision and a standard for all places and all times.

First Reading

I

If you have read the Reading Plan entitled *A General Introduction to the Great Books,* you may recall that one of the readings was from Plato's *Republic.* In fact, that reading overlaps this one, since it includes both Books I and II. On the other hand, this may be your first acquaintance with the *Republic.* In either case, you will have no difficulty if you start with Book II.

The reason for the overlap and for starting with Book II is that this Reading Plan concentrates on the subject of politics. Books II-V deal primarily with political matters: the origin and organization of a state; the education of its ruling and warrior classes; the role of women in the state. Book I, on the other hand, is mainly concerned with the question, "What is justice?"

The discussion of justice carries over into Book II. The dialogue turns from the subject of justice to that of the state because Socrates suggests that he and the other persons in the dialogue will have an easier time understanding what a just man is if they first can see what a just state is. Since a state is larger than a man, it will be easier to see an attribute like justice in the state than in man. Speaking to Adeimantus, Socrates says:

. . . justice, which is the subject of our enquiry, is, as you know, sometimes spoken of as the virtue of an individual, and sometimes as the virtue of a State.

True, he replied.

And is not a State larger than an individual?

It is.

Then in the larger the quantity of justice is likely to be larger and more easily discernible. I propose therefore that we enquire into the nature of justice and injustice, first as they appear in the State, and secondly in the individual, proceeding from the greater to the lesser and comparing them. (Book II, p. 316b)

If, therefore, you have already read Book II, or if you want to shorten the reading assignment, page 316b would be a good place to start. This does not mean that justice does not belong in a discussion of politics. On the contrary, it is definitely a political matter for Plato; indeed, if politics were not concerned with justice (*i.e.*, if the state were not concerned with justice), Socrates would surely be wrong in attempting to discover the nature of justice by looking at the state.

II

Before turning to the content of the *Republic*, let us spend a little time on its structure. It is a dialogue, as all of Plato's writings are, except for a few letters (see the Seventh Letter at the end of Volume 7). A dialogue is a conversation between two or more persons.

Socrates is usually the main speaker in Plato's dialogues. In some dialogues, however, such as the *Parmenides* and the *Sophist*, he is not the major person, and in the *Laws* he does not appear at all. The *Apology*, though always grouped with the dialogues, is really a series of speeches by Socrates.

There is great variation in the way Plato stages his drama. In some pieces he presents the kind of a dialogue a playwright would write. He indicates the scene briefly, and gives each person in the dialogue speeches to say. The *Crito* is an example of this simple, dramatic kind of dialogue. In the *Phaedo* the picture is slightly more complicated: Phaedo *narrates* the dialogue to Echecrates, so that the "action" of the dialogue is somewhat more remote from us.

In the *Republic*, too, Plato uses the device of having someone narrate the dialogue, sometime after it took place. In this case, however, Socrates himself is the narrator so that what the dialogue loses in directness it gains in authenticity, since presumably Socrates would know best what was said, and especially what he himself said. The persons to whom Socrates narrates the dialogue are not named; however, in the *Timaeus*, it is made clear that the same persons are present as were present at the recitation of the *Republic*. Socrates remarks to Timaeus, Critias, and Hermocrates that on the previous day he discoursed on the state. He then gives a brief summary of what he said about the state. His summary covers just about Books II-V of the *Republic*. You may want to glance at this summary, after you finish your reading; it is found on pp. 442b-443b of Volume 7.

For an example of how complicated Plato's method of putting various middlemen between the persons of the dialogue and the reader can become, take a look at the first page of the *Parmenides*. It takes quite a bit of untangling before it is clear who reports what to whom. The original dialogue is mainly between Parmenides, Zeno, and Socrates; it took place a long time before the retelling of it. Pythodorus recounted the dialogue to Antiphon, Antiphon in turn told it to Cephalus, and Cephalus is the one into whose mouth Plato puts the words which we finally read. Thus instead of directly reporting the words of Socrates, Parmenides, and Zeno, Plato chooses to report the words of Cephalus, who must be understood as saying things like this (taking the first words of Socrates on p. 487a as the example): "Antiphon said that Pythodorus said that Socrates said: 'What is your meaning, Zeno?' "

Although Plato does not use the clumsy device of "Antiphon said that Pythodorus said that Socrates said . . .," but proceeds *as if* directly reporting the speeches of Socrates, Parmenides, and Zeno, the fact remains that he chooses to put three persons, Cephalus, Antiphon, and Pythodorus, between the reader and the speakers of the dialogue proper. This sort of thing is hardly accidental. If we may guess at what it means, it seems as though Plato, while he is the author of this dialogue, wishes to take as little responsibility as possible for what is being said in it. By making the dialogue take place years before it is reported, and by putting three intermediaries between speaker and reader, he practically invites the suggestion that the dialogue may have been garbled, and that its written form is in many ways not like the original spoken form. Any errors, inconsistencies, impieties, etc., could be easily ascribed to these conditions of transmittal.

Plato's intention in the *Republic* may be just the opposite. The narrator placed between the reader and the speakers of the dialogue is Socrates, the chief person of the dialogue. This device also decreases Plato's responsibility for the dialogue, though less so than in the case of the *Parmenides*, but it increases Socrates' responsibility, for he himself narrates what he said. It is as if Plato were answering, by this device, the question: "How much in this dialogue is Socratic theory, and how much is Platonic theory?" "It is at least one stage removed from me," Plato seems to be saying, "but it is a very Socratic theory indeed."

III

While it would be tedious to indicate in great detail the structure of these four books, it may be helpful to give some indication of how topic follows upon topic. If you fail to pay close attention to the organization of a Platonic dialogue, it sometimes seems to develop haphazardly, as if Plato simply jumps from point to point. Actually, the *Republic* is a well-knit piece, with hardly any loose ends. If we start at page 316b, we may analyze the dialogue as follows:

1. Genetic development of the state.	316b-319a
2. Origin of war. The warrior class.	
The character of the warriors.	319a-320c
3. The education of the warriors.	320c-339a
a. Music: what should and should not be taught in the arts.	320d-334b
(1) Content.	320d-328b
(2) Style.	328b-331c
(3) Melody and song.	331c-333b
b. Gymnastic.	334b-339a
4. The guardians, the ruling class of the state. Their character, life, duties, and rewards.	339a-346a
5. The nature of justice and injustice.	346a-356a
a. Wisdom.	346c-347a
b. Courage.	347a-347d
c. Temperance.	347d-348d

IV

So far we have been concerned mainly with the form and structure of the *Republic* and have paid very little attention to its content. But, of course, any reader of the dialogue must face the question: "Is what it says true or at least plausible? And if so, what are the arguments to support its contentions?"

1. The nature of justice. Our first concern naturally will be to find out the result of the quest for justice. Has Socrates made good his promise to discover justice first in the state and then in the individual? We find the answer in Book IV.

After Socrates has described his imaginary state, and its division into three classes, he discovers four virtues and links them to political functions. The first is wisdom, the virtue appropriate to the guardian class. The second is courage, the virtue appropriate to the warrior class. The third is temperance, "the agreement of the naturally superior and inferior, as to the right to rule of either, both in states and in individuals." The fourth is justice; but, Socrates maintains, justice has already been discovered:

You remember the original principle which we were always laying down at the foundation of the State, that one man should practise one thing only, the thing to which his nature was best adapted—now justice is this principle or a part of it . . .

Further, we affirmed that justice was doing one's own business, and not being a busybody; we said so again and again, and many others have said the same to us . . .

Then to do one's own business in a certain way may be assumed to be justice . . .

. . . I think that this is the only virtue which remains in the State when the other virtues of temperance and courage and wisdom are abstracted; and, that this is the ultimate cause and condition of the existence of all of them, and while remaining in them is also their preservative; and we are saying that if the three were discovered by us, justice would be the fourth or remaining one. (p. 349a-b)

Socrates sums up his view of justice once more by saying

. . . when the trader, the auxiliary, and the guardian each do their own business, that is justice, and will make the city just. (p. 350a)

So much for the just state. It still remains to be shown how the discovery of justice in the state can help us find what makes a man just. Socrates accomplishes the transition from state to individual by showing that just as in the state there are three classes, so in the individual person there are three principles. They are reason, passion, and appetite. Now the conclusion is easily drawn:

The individual will be acknowledged by us to be just in the same way in which the State is just . . .

We cannot but remember that the justice of the State consisted in each of the three classes doing the work of its own class . . .

We must recollect that the individual in whom the several qualities of his nature do their own work will be just, and will do his own work . . . (pp. 353d-354a)

Socrates summarizes his view of justice once more in a long paragraph, on pp. 354d-355b, which you may now want to reread.

2. Community of women and children. Perhaps the best-known and most notorious proposal that Plato makes for his ideal state is that the guardians should have their wives and children in common. Plato introduces the subject in a very offhand manner. He mentions it in passing in Book IV (p. 344b) remarking that, of course, marriage and children will be in common because "friends have all things in common."

Though the remark is at first ignored, Adeimantus returns to it a few pages later (p. 356c), commenting that in the matter of women and children it is by no means self-evident that "friends have all things in common." Socrates still does not give any arguments for his view; instead he shows that men and women should be equal in tasks and education. And when the question of the community of women and children comes up again (p. 360b), he decides once more to postpone the consideration of how such a plan is possible and what can be said in its support; instead he describes the arrangements that are involved in such a plan. Finally, however, Socrates faces the issue:

And now you would have the argument show that this community is consistent with the rest of our polity, and also that nothing can be better—would you not? . . . What ought to be the chief aim of the legislator in making laws and in the organization of a State—what is the greatest good, and what is the greatest evil? . . . Can there be any greater evil than discord and distraction and plurality where unity ought to reign? or any greater good than the bond of unity? . . . And there is unity where there is community of pleasures and pains—where all the citizens are glad or grieved on the same occasions of joy and sorrow . . . Where there is no common but only private feeling a State is disorganized—when you have one half of the world triumphing and the other plunged in grief at the same events happening to the city or the citizens . . . Such differences commonly originate in a disagreement about the use of the terms "mine" and "not mine," "his" and "not his" . . . And is not that the best-ordered State in which the greatest number of persons apply the terms "mine" and "not mine" in the same way to the same thing? (Book V, p. 363b-c)

And Socrates concludes the argument as follows:

Then in our city the language of harmony and concord will be more often heard than in any other . . . And agreeably to this mode of thinking and speaking, were we not saying that [the guardians] will have their pleasures and pains in common? . . . And they will have a common interest in the same thing which they will alike call "my own," and having this common interest they will have a common feeling of pleasure and pain? . . . And the reason of this, over and above the general constitution of the State, will be that the guardians will have a community of women and children? . . . And this unity of feeling we admitted to be the greatest good . . . Then the community of wives and children among our citizens is clearly the source of the greatest good to the State? (Book V, p. 364b-c)

Summed up in a sentence, the argument comes to this: "The community of women and children is good, because it promotes the unity of the State."

3. The "royal lie." Another argument of Socrates that deserves attention because it is so unusual occurs in Book III,

pp. 340b-341a. After first introducing the ruling or guardian class, Socrates proposes a "royal lie" to make the existence of higher classes more palatable to the lower classes. "How," Socrates asks,

may we devise one of those needful falsehoods of which we lately spoke—just one royal lie which may deceive the rulers, if that be possible, and at any rate the rest of the city?

Socrates answers his own question:

Citizens, we shall say to them in our tale, you are brothers, yet God has framed you differently. Some of you have the power of command, and in the composition of these he has mingled gold, wherefore also they have the greatest honour; others he has made of silver, to be auxiliaries; others again who are to be husbandmen and craftsmen he has composed of brass and iron; and the species will generally be preserved in the children. But as all are of the same original stock, a golden parent will sometimes have a silver son, or a silver parent a golden son . . . If the son of a golden or silver parent has an admixture of brass and iron, then nature orders a transposition of ranks, and the eye of the ruler must not be pitiful towards the child because he has to descend in the scale and become a husbandman or artisan, just as there may be sons of artisans who having an admixture of gold or silver in them are raised to honour, and become guardians or auxiliaries.

And the reason for this strict attention to the quality of the offspring is that

an oracle says that when a man of brass or iron guards the State, it will be destroyed.

Neither Socrates nor his hearers have much confidence that this royal lie will be believed. But they appear to find nothing morally wrong in trying to fool the people with it. Thus we find the telling of lies advocated in a work devoted to the investigation of the nature of justice, even if it is only one kind of lie, to be told for special reasons and under special circumstances.

V

We may raise some serious questions about these passages:

Is Plato's argument for the community of women and children sound?

Is unity in the state the greatest good? Furthermore, granted that unity is at least *a* good, will the community of women and children promote it?

Nobody will deny that there must be some unity in a state; otherwise the citizens would not live in a state, but as an accidental collection of people. But there is such a thing as too much unity in a state. Unity may not be an unqualified good, nor the greatest good in the state. For example, would not a dictatorship, a "totalitarian" state, enjoy the greatest unity? How, in other words, can Plato prevent his state from becoming so unified as to infringe on individual liberty?

We may say the same thing the other way around: Is not diversity in a state also good? For instance, democracy in the United States works on the assumption that a wide variety of institutions and opinions is good. In fact, could not the United States Bill of Rights be summed up as saying: "Each citizen has the right to be as different from other citizens as he pleases, within very wide limits?"

But even if we grant Plato's premise that unity in the state is desirable, there is great doubt that community of wives and children would promote it. Would it not be the case, instead, that no one would pay attention to the business of educating the children or providing for the women, since each would assume that someone else would take care of it? Or again, why does Plato not consider the argument that each one loves best and is most concerned over what is his own? In fact, one could argue convincingly that no man can be happy without some private property or something that is just *his*—without this he becomes lost and anonymous, and loses his distinctness from other men.

Both criticisms—that unity is not necessarily good for the state, and that community of women and children does not necessarily promote unity—are advanced by Aristotle. He considers both points in the *Politics:* the first in Book II, Chapter 2, and the second in Chapter 3.

Is it just to tell a "royal lie"?

We cannot avoid asking this question of Plato. There certainly are some moralists (for example, Immanuel Kant) who maintain that it is never right to tell a lie. Other writers agree that it is sometimes justifiable to tell a lie; for instance, in order to prevent a greater injustice from being done. Presumably, we may lie concerning the whereabouts of a friend if a man with obviously murderous intentions asks us where the friend is.

But is Plato's "royal lie" of this sort? What is the great injustice being prevented? One answer which Plato might give is "the destruction of the state." But even if we accept the preservation of the state as a very worthy end, is it more important than truthtelling? Here it must be remembered that the "royal lie" is not just a little, unimportant, one-time lie; on the contrary, it has to be told over and over again. And its purpose is to assign people to different classes, without their grumbling. We may put the question to Plato in this form: "Is the preservation of the state so important that for its sake some men are to be permanently denied the opportunity of bettering themselves, of rising from the artisan class, for instance, to the warrior class? Who is to judge that a man is of brass and iron? And how can we be sure that no mistakes are made?" Sentiment in the United States in modern times would consider individual growth and development at least as important as the maintenance of the *status quo* in the state.

Yet another troublesome question faces Plato if he admits that the royal lie is an injustice, though a lesser one than the one he tries to prevent by it. What becomes of the doctrine— so vigorously defended in Books I and II of the *Republic*— that it is better to suffer an injustice than to commit one? Here Plato seems to reverse his stand. And if he should answer that moral principles sometimes have to be changed for the sake of practical considerations, does that not overthrow any possibility of having fixed moral principles at all?

Could a state like that envisioned in the Republic ever actually come into existence?

Plato answers this question in what is perhaps the most famous passage in the first five books.

> Until philosophers are kings, or the kings and princes of this world have the spirit and power of philosophy, and political greatness and wisdom meet in one, and those commoner natures who pursue either to the exclusion of the other are compelled to stand aside, cities will never have rest from their evils—no, nor the human race, as I believe—and then only will our State have a possibility of life and behold the light of day. (p. 369d)

What does Plato mean by a philosopher-king? He must mean more than simply a ruler who also is learned in philosophy. History shows us some examples of such rulers; yet none of them were able to even approximate a state like Plato's. The Roman Empire, for instance, was ruled for many years by Marcus Aurelius Antoninus, who was also a famous Stoic philosopher. (His *Meditations* are included in Volume 12 of this set.) And while Marcus Aurelius was an excellent emperor, he failed so far in wisdom and political sense that he chose as his successor his son Commodus (custom permitted the emperor to choose anyone as his successor), a man so entirely opposite to his father that, in Gibbon's words, "the monstrous vices of the son have cast a shade on the purity of the father's virtues."

Plato, therefore, means a union of the philosopher's and the statesman's virtues that must be sufficiently deep so that all of the political acts of the philosopher-king are wise, and so that all his philosophical thought is directed toward political ends. Here, of course, we must ask Plato whether such a union is possible. Not only must we question the practical possibility of ever finding a philosopher-king (for Plato would be quick enough to agree that such a possibility is very slight); we must also ask Plato and ourselves whether there is not perhaps an intrinsic incompatibility between the two kinds of virtues.

Is it possible, in other words, to be a successful and good

statesman and still be a philosopher? Or does the pursuit of philosophy require a more quiet and remote sort of life? And conversely, will not a philosopher have to fail as a statesman, just because he is a philosopher? Perhaps this particular mixture of greatness in practical affairs as well as in theoretical speculation is simply not possible.

Plato repeatedly makes the point that things should not be changed (out of desire to improve or adorn them) to such an extent that they cease to be what they are meant to be; for instance, it would be ridiculous to change the guardians' life (out of desire to make it more pleasurable) so much that they could no longer be guardians. Must perhaps a statesman who is also a philosopher cease to be a statesman, while similarly a philosopher who is also a statesman must cease to be a philosopher?

We hope that the answer to the last question is No; yet there is much historical evidence in favor of the affirmative answer, and a negative answer would certainly require an elaborate and cogent argument.

The following questions are designed to help you test the thoroughness of your reading. Each question is to be answered by giving a page or pages of the reading assignment. Answers will be found on page 219 of this Reading Plan.

1 What is the nature of courage in the state?

2 What is the nature of wisdom in the state?

3 What story does Socrates tell to show that passion or spirit is a third element in the human soul in addition to reason and desire?

4 What is the story of the ring of Gyges?

5 What is the state that Glaucon calls "the city of pigs"?

6 What is Socrates' opinion with respect to lying (other than telling "the royal lie")?

7 Is Socrates concerned with the happiness of the state or the happiness of individuals?

8 What is the most important thing for the health and preservation of the state?

9 Do the guardians have any private property?

10 What does Plato say about enslaving conquered peoples?

ARISTOTLE

Politics
Books III–IV

Vol. 9, pp. 471–502

Also, ARISTOTLE

Politics
Book I

Vol. 9, pp. 445–455

For a discussion of this assignment,
see the Fifth Reading in

A General Introduction to the Great Books

Often when we read the writers of the past we feel
that their experience and their way of looking at things
is entirely different from our own. But when Aristotle
talks about politics and the problems of government,
we feel at home with his approach and familiar with
the issues he raises. His espousal of constitutional government, for example, recalls certain trends in our own
political history.

Aristotle's realistic appraisal of political actualities
also has a modern touch. His awareness of the various
temptations open to man as a political animal finds a

response in us, who have lived through all kinds of political cataclysms and perversities. We know, of course, that Aristotle is no mere neutral describer of facts. He does not believe that whatever is is right. He knows that perversion of the true forms and ends of government is one of the tragic possibilities of politics, and that it occurs again and again. Aristotle gives us a pathology of political life. Mob rule and self-centered despotism figure as the worst diseases in this pathology.

Can we apply Aristotle's analysis to twentieth-century politics? For instance, he sees tyranny as the lawless rule of one man over unwilling subjects, with the good of the ruler as the main aim. This definition seems to fit the regimes of Hitler and Stalin, which were certainly lawless and unjust. But were their subjects unwilling and was self-aggrandizement their main motivation? Are modern tyrannies exactly like the ones Aristotle was acquainted with in antiquity? When we try to apply Aristotle's analysis we may find that it fits some modern conditions and not others. Both findings can help us to become aware of the present shape of things.

Second Reading

I

Plato wrote three dialogues that are primarily political in character: the *Republic, Statesman,* and *Laws.* From your acquaintance with the *Republic* you know that it is concerned —mainly, though by no means entirely—with the nature of the ideal state. The *Statesman* (sometimes called *Politicus*) deals, of course, with the nature and virtue of a king or statesman. The *Laws,* finally, represents Plato's last and most mature thought on the rules and ordinances that are to govern the best state; there is less emphasis here than in the *Republic* on the ideal character of such a state. In the *Laws* Plato tries to come to grips with particular and down-to-earth problems of legislation.

Aristotle deals with all three problems—the nature of the ideal state, the nature of the statesman, the nature of the best state—in one work, the *Politics.* While the First Reading dealt with Plato's ideal state, this reading has to do with Aristotle's view of states as they are; and when, in the latter part of Book IV, he speaks of the best state, he has in mind something much less lofty than Plato's republic.

Aristotle's own view of the ideal state comes later, in Books VII and VIII. However, in Book II of the *Politics* he considers ideal commonwealths that have been imagined by various writers, including Plato. The first five chapters of Book II are given over to a criticism of the *Republic,* and, with the relevant parts of Plato's work fresh in mind, you may wish to add these chapters to your reading. We have already, in the guide to the First Reading, touched on some of Aristotle's criticisms.

You may, of course, wonder why we do not follow up the

reading of the *Republic* with the last books of the *Politics,* thereby making possible a comparison between Plato's and Aristotle's version of the ideal state. In part the reason is that it is always better to read earlier parts of a book before later ones. Although it seems possible to skip Book II of the *Politics* without impairing too much the sense of continuity and unity of the book, it would hardly be easy to jump to Book VII. Too much of what has been said in the earlier books is assumed there. Secondly, in Plato's writing the construction of the ideal state, as outlined in the *Republic,* is exciting reading; in Aristotle's work, on the other hand, his genius shines forth most brilliantly when he discusses possible and existing states, and their organization and operation.

It may be of some interest here to recall that both Plato and Aristotle ventured to put their political thoughts into practice. Plato's failure and Aristotle's partial success in practical politics might be explained by Plato's bent for the ideal and Aristotle's penchant for the actual.

Plato tells us about his political ventures in the Seventh Letter (see Vol. 7, pp. 800-814). He made two trips to Syracuse (the first one in the year 367 B.C., when Aristotle began to attend the Platonic Academy) for the purpose of educating its young ruler, Dionysius. Though Plato had considerable misgivings about the trip, he felt that he could not afford to pass up this opportunity of putting into practice his ideas about laws and constitutions. However, instead of succeeding in making a philosopher-king out of Dionysius, Plato very quickly became involved in the intrigues of the Syracusan court. Dionysius was apparently more interested in using Plato as a pawn in his political machinations than in learning from him; and after his second visit, Plato was permitted to return to Athens only with some difficulty.

Aristotle, as we know from Plutarch, also took a hand in the education of a ruler. For several years Alexander the Great came under his influence. How much Aristotle actually contributed to Alexander's education and to what extent Alexander followed his teachings is not altogether clear. Plutarch, who is quite trustworthy in these matters, has this to say:

For a while he [Alexander] loved and cherished Aristotle no less, as he was wont to say himself, than if he had been his father, giving this reason for it, that as he had received life from the one, so the other had taught him to live well. But afterwards, upon some mistrust of him, yet not so great as to make him do him any hurt, his familiarity and friendly kindness to him abated so much of its former force and affectionateness, as to make it evident he was alienated from him. However, his violent thirst after and passion for learning, which were once implanted, still grew up with him, and never decayed . . . (Vol. 14, p. 544a)

Thus Aristotle's excursion into the education of princes was also not without disappointment. Nevertheless, Alexander remains as a more worthy monument to Aristotle's teaching than Dionysius does to Plato's.

II

At the beginning of the *Politics*, as at the beginning of each of Aristotle's works in these translations, there is an analytical table of contents. By looking at it, you can easily discern the main divisions of Books III and IV. But it will nevertheless be convenient to point out some of the high lights of these two books.

Aristotle begins Book III by answering the question, "What is a citizen?" He defines a citizen thus:

He who has the power to take part in the deliberative or judicial administration of any state is said by us to be a citizen of that state; and, speaking generally, a state is a body of citizens sufficing for the purposes of life. (p. 472c)

Notice that with this definition there will necessarily be far fewer citizens than inhabitants of a state. For example, slaves, women, and children reside in a state without being citizens. All of these benefit from living in the state, even though they are not citizens. In this respect, Aristotle's view differs hardly at all from our common contemporary view; until recently we excluded women from citizenship (in Aristotle's sense), and we still exclude children, felons, the insane, and foreigners. Nowadays, of course, the word "citizen" is often used simply to refer to residents of a state; in that sense women, children, etc., are citizens. But for Aristotle citizenship is a kind of office; its duties are those of "deliberative or judicial administration." Here again (if we ignore the trivial meaning of citizen as resident) there is great similarity to the modern situation. Citizenship nowadays confers the right to vote and to hold office. The citizens exercise the deliberative function indirectly by electing representatives. They exercise the judicial function, insofar as that can be done by laymen, through jury service—it is from among the voters that jurors are drawn.

The main difference between Aristotle's views and those that prevail in modern industrial democracy arises with the question, "Who shall be admitted to citizenship?" Aristotle, as a matter of course, excludes slaves and women, while we deny that any man should be a slave and have, in the twentieth century, enfranchised women. But Aristotle goes further. He asks

Is he only a true citizen who has a share of office, or is the mechanic to be included? . . . And if none of the lower class are citizens, in which part of the state are they to be placed? For they are not resident aliens, and they are not foreigners. May we not reply, that . . . there is no more absurdity in excluding them than in excluding slaves and freedmen? . . . It must be admitted that we cannot consider all those to be citizens who are necessary to the existence of the state; for example, children are not citizens equally, with grown-up men . . . (Book III, Ch. 5, p. 475a)

Thus Aristotle seems to be on the verge of saying that only men belonging to the upper or leisure classes are true citizens. Here we can see a difference between Aristotle's and Plato's treatment of politics. Whereas Plato was only concerned with the ideal state and its citizens, Aristotle's treatment is partly historical and concerned with existing rather than perfect states. Thus, Aristotle, instead of concentrating on the "true" citizen, goes on as follows:

Since there are many forms of government there must be many varieties of citizens, and especially of citizens who are subjects; so that under some governments the mechanic and the labourer will be citizens, but not in others, as, for example, in aristocracy or the so-called government of the best (if there be such an one), in which honours are given according to virtue and merit; for no man can practise virtue who is living the life of a mechanic or labourer. (Book III, Ch. 5, p. 475b-c)

Aristotle is willing to concede the title "citizen" to whoever is admitted to the deliberative and judicial function. At the same time, Aristotle clearly thinks (according to the last sentence above) that in popular forms of government the citizens include men of no virtue or merit.

In fact, in Chapter 4 of Book III Aristotle raises just this problem: "Does a citizen have to be virtuous?" We must consider, he writes, "Whether the virtue of a good man and a good citizen is the same or not." As we have seen, the answer must be "No," since in many states a laborer can be a good citizen, while, according to Aristotle, such a man cannot be virtuous. At the same time, of course, a good citizen *may* also be a good man; and there is one case where the good citizen is required to be a good man. This occurs when the citizen is to be not merely a subject but a ruler. It is not possible, according to Aristotle, to be a good ruler without also being a good man.

III

Aristotle next discusses the various forms of government. The main question here is which are the just and which the unjust forms of government. Aristotle answers the question neatly:

Governments which have a regard to the common interest are constituted in accordance with strict principles of justice, and are therefore true forms; but those which regard only the interest of the rulers are all defective and perverted forms, for they are despotic, whereas a state is a community of freemen. (Book III, Ch. 6, p. 476c)

This echoes Aristotle's remarks in the first book of the *Politics*. There he says:

the rule of a master is not a constitutional rule, and . . . all the different kinds of rule are not, as some affirm, the same with each other. For there is one rule exercised over subjects who are by nature free, another over subjects who are by nature slaves. The rule of a household is a monarchy, for every house is under one head: whereas constitutional rule is a government of freemen and equals. (Book I, Ch. 7, p. 449b)

Just forms of government, therefore, are *constitutional*.

The two main constitutional forms of government are oligarchy and democracy. The main dispute both in Greek history and in political theory has always been that between a government of the poor (who are many) and a government of the rich (who are few).

For the real difference between democracy and oligarchy is poverty and wealth. Wherever men rule by reason of their wealth, whether they be few or many, that is an oligarchy, and where the poor rule, that is a democracy. But as a fact the rich are few and the poor many; for few are well-to-do, whereas freedom is enjoyed by all, and wealth and freedom are the grounds on which the oligarchical and democratical parties respectively claim power in the state. (Book III, Ch. 8, p. 477b-c)

The oligarchic and democratic constitutions each claim to be based on justice; but their view of justice is different. The oligarchs maintain that there is inequality between those who own property and those who do not. Hence it is just, they say, that all those who are equal in being property owners should be treated equally, *i.e.*, should be rulers. On the other hand, those who are unequal to them because they do not own property (the majority of the populace) should be treated unequally; *i.e.*, should be ruled.

The democrats, on the other hand, maintain that those who are equal in respect of free birth (every citizen) should all be treated equally and be permitted to rule. Both oligarchs and democrats, therefore, base their claims on justice and agree that equals should be treated equally and unequals, unequally; but they differ radically on the qualifications with respect to which equality and inequality are to be measured (see Book III, Chapter 9).

These are the general principles on which democracy and oligarchy are based. In Book IV, Chapter 4-6, Aristotle considers the various subtypes of these constitutions. Both democracy and oligarchy admit of degrees. In each case, too, Aristotle points out that the principle of the constitution may be pushed to an extreme. Democracies may become so extreme that men (the masses) rather than laws rule, resulting in demagoguery and mob rule. Similarly, oligarchies may become so extreme that all power is concentrated in the hands of a few families and again, men (from these families) rather than laws rule, resulting in despotism or tyranny.

IV

Although Aristotle's treatment is straightforward, it is also rather condensed, and it may be well to ask ourselves a few questions in order to appreciate fully all the implications of his views.

What is the difference between the virtue of a good man and the virtue of a citizen?

To help us answer the question, let us look at two sentences. One we have already quoted:

He who has the power to take part in the deliberative or judicial administration of any state is said by us to be a citizen of that state. (Book III, Ch. 1, p. 472c)

And consider also this one:

If the state cannot be entirely composed of good men, . . . the virtue of the citizen and of the good man cannot coincide. All must have the virtue of the good citizen—thus, and thus only, can the state be perfect; but they will not have the virtue of a good man, unless we assume that in the good state all the citizens must be good. (Book III, Ch. 4, pp. 473d-474a)

Clearly the virtue of the good man must be a greater thing than the virtue of the citizen. For instance, someone might be called a virtuous man if he possessed all of the so-called "cardinal virtues." These are the four virtues which Plato enumerates in the *Republic,* while Socrates is trying to discover justice. They are courage, temperance, wisdom, and justice. The good man should have at least those three of these virtues that Aristotle himself enumerates as moral virtues in the *Nicomachean Ethics,* viz., courage, temperance, and justice.

Evidently, Aristotle thinks that the good citizen can get along without some or all of these virtues. Yet it is difficult to see how. How can the citizen "take part in the deliberative or judicial administration" unless he possesses the virtues of wisdom, temperance, and justice? Nor must he be lacking in courage, if military service is one of the duties of the citizen.

Aristotle does not simply say that a *citizen* need not be a good man; he maintains that a *good citizen* need not be a good man (*i.e.*, need not have the virtue of a good man). The question then becomes: How can a man be a good citizen—which means to fulfill the functions of a citizen well, to deliberate and adjudicate well—without possessing the moral or cardinal virtues?

In another context, Aristotle makes some remarks that may be applicable here. The problem is how to defend the view that the multitude (*i.e.*, all or most of the citizens) ought to be supreme rather than the few best men. He explains:

> The many, of whom each individual is but an ordinary person, when they meet together may very likely be better than the few good, if regarded not individually but collectively, just as a feast to which many contribute is better than a dinner provided out of a single purse. For each individual among the many has a share of virtue and prudence, and when they meet together, they become in a manner one man . . . (Book III, Ch. 11, p. 479b)

If this is to be Aristotle's answer, however, should he not have added, when saying that the good citizen need not have the full or perfect virtue of a good man, that he must have some beginnings of such virtue? For unless each citizen has some virtue, how can they all together be better than a good man?

Is the election of officials by lot rather than by vote defensible?

If none of the citizens needs to be extraordinarily good, it follows that in a democracy in Aristotle's sense (where all the citizens are rulers in turn) none of the rulers is extraordinarily good. And since each citizen, we said above, has to have some little share of virtue, it also follows that none of the citizens is extraordinarily bad. It is perhaps some such reasoning that led to the custom of appointing officials in a democracy by lot rather than vote. If any citizen is eligible for office, and if all citizens are equally removed from full virtue or vice, it would seem to make no difference who is elected. Hence, the reasoning goes, election by lot is as good a way as any (see Book IV, Chapter 15).

Since election by lot is no longer practiced in modern democracies, we may wonder about the cogency of this reasoning. First, however, it may be well to see whether we can discern any advantages in this method. Is it an advantage, for instance, that all political campaigns would be eliminated? Again, politics as a profession would be eliminated, since no one could deliberately run for office. We often use the word "politics" as a term of opprobrium; would the elimination of "politics" be good? Both of these questions seem capable of answers that would be partially affirmative and partially negative.

But furthermore, is it not wasteful to assume that a democracy never produces any outstanding men? If, indeed, all the citizens of a democracy were complete mediocrities, election by lot might be suitable; but is it not more likely that some men will be, at least in some respects, better than their fellows? And how, under chance selection, will there be any opportunity for political expertness to develop? Incidentally, it seems only fair to point out that Aristotle does not advocate election by lot for democracies; he merely records that in many democracies at least some of the offices were filled in this way.

What conditions of property ownership promote the best kind of state?

In Book IV, Chapter 11, Aristotle considers what is the best form of government. In the middle of the chapter he writes as follows:

Thus it is manifest that the best political community is formed by citizens of the middle class, and that those states are likely to be well-administered, in which the middle class is large, and stronger if possible than both the other classes, or at any rate than either singly; for the addition of the middle class turns the scale, and prevents either of the extremes from being dominant. Great then is the good fortune of a state in which the citizens have a moderate and sufficient property; for where some possess much, and the others nothing, there may arise an extreme democracy, or a pure oligarchy; or a tyranny may grow out of either extreme,—either out of the most rampant democracy, or out of an oligarchy; but it is not so likely to arise out of the middle constitutions and those akin to them. (p. 496a-b)

Two questions are suggested by this passage. One is: "Which

is the best form of government?" The paragraph above does not seem to give an unequivocal answer. Perhaps it is not a question that can be answered unequivocally. The second question takes off directly from the paragraph quoted: "What is the relation between forms of government and economic conditions?" Is one form of government especially well suited for one economic condition and another form for another condition? Or is the form of government a necessary function of the economic situation? Aristotle certainly relates the political and economic factors. Here we should note that Karl Marx asserted that political and economic conditions are *necessarily* related. How much do Aristotle and Marx agree and differ?

What are the rights, duties, and privileges of citizenship?

Let us consider this question in terms of the United States today. Does a citizen have any duties at all? He may have duties from a moral point of view, but it is hard to find any legally enforceable duties. A United States citizen is anyone who is born in the United States or who has been naturalized. Such a person is entitled to all the rights and privileges of citizenship. But if a citizen does not register as a voter, he cannot be charged with any political functions. If he does register as a voter, then he may be required to serve as a juror at some time or other. The exercise of the franchise is, therefore, connected with at least this duty.

Of course, certain other things are required by the state. For instance, men may be required to serve in the armed forces. This, however, is not a duty of citizenship in the strictest sense. It is rather an instance of what *may* be such a duty, viz., that of obeying the duly made laws. We see that service in the armed forces is not tied to citizenship since men who are too young to vote and resident aliens are required to serve.

The question naturally suggests itself, whether this is a good state of affairs. Should not the rights of citizenship be tied to the performance of duties? Plans have been suggested, for example, to make voting compulsory and to punish those citizens who fail to vote by fining them. It has also been suggested that voting be rewarded; for instance, that voters be paid for the exercise of their franchise. This, of course, might well increase the percentage of citizens who vote, but it would not make voting an obligatory duty. On the contrary, it would appear to emphasize the optional character of this function. A person might choose to lose money rather than to vote. Only dictatorships are able to compel nearly all eligible persons to vote.

The following questions are designed to help you test the thoroughness of your reading. Each question is to be answered by giving a page or pages of the reading assignment. Answers will be found on page 219 of this Reading Plan.

1 What is Aristotle's most comprehensive definition of a citizen?

2 What does Aristotle say the constitution is?

3 What is the correct definition of an oligarchy?

4 What are the considerations that are relevant with respect to qualification for holding office?

5 What is the justification for ostracism?

6 What is a democracy according to Aristotle?

7 What are the different kinds of democracy? the kinds of oligarchy?

8 What is the general nature of polity or constitutional government?

9 What two things are required for good government?

PLUTARCH

The Lives of the Noble Grecians and Romans

"Agis," "Cleomenes," "Tiberius Gracchus,"
"Caius Gracchus," "Caius and Tiberius Gracchus
and Agis and Cleomenes Compared"

Vol. 14, pp. 648–691

So far we have looked at politics through the eyes
of philosophers. Now we turn from Plato's soaring
idealism and Aristotle's detached analysis to Plutarch's
vivid portrayal of the great leaders of ancient Greece
and Rome. This master recreator of character and
situation makes the past live again for us as he portrays
these historic personages in their greatness and
weakness.

Political and social ideas which may have been
remote abstractions for us now take on life. From
Plato we got the image of an ideal state, from Aristotle
the insight that the conflict of the rich and the poor
is a permanent feature of political life. In the present
reading, we see what actually happened in Sparta
when two young, idealistic kings tried to restore the
virtue, austerity, and glory of olden times. Their efforts
to divide land equally and cancel debts met the im-

placable opposition of the wealthy classes. The lives of both kings ended in tragic and violent deaths, one by legal lynching, the other by suicide. Plutarch also tells us the parallel story of two brothers from a noble family in Rome who became leaders of the common people and sponsored a program of social reforms. They, too, met the opposition of the wealthy and well-born. One of them was lynched by a mob of senators. The other escaped a similar fate by suicide.

As Plutarch tells these stories, they are tales of weakness as well as of virtue on both sides. He treats human failings with pity and understanding. His creative vision gives us the whole picture: idealism and vanity, devotion and cupidity, mercy and cruelty, sometimes together in the same man. Plutarch shows us right and justice operative in public affairs; he also shows us vote stealing, logrolling, and campaign oratory. The political idealists use force, terror, and fraud to gain their ends. A mob of the wellborn and well-to-do lynch the social reformer. But Plutarch does not merely present the facts of political life. He is not a reporter but a poet who sees tragedy in the character and destiny of these men. He gives us the depths as well as the surface of political reality.

Third Reading

I

Plutarch's *Lives* are also called *Parallel Lives,* because Plutarch usually follows the life of a famous Greek with that of a famous Roman, and then compares the two men. (Sometimes, to be sure, the extant text lacks the comparison, or even one of the parallel lives.) In the present reading, however, two Greeks —both Spartan kings—are compared with two Roman brothers. Plutarch sees a parallel between the Gracchi brothers and Agis and Cleomenes, who "were not indeed brothers by nature, . . . but . . . had a kind of brotherly resemblance in their actions and designs" (p. 649b-c).

Plutarch's main concern is with human virtue and vice. Our own interest here is in what these four lives have to say about politics. We find that they shed interesting light on our previous readings. The Spartan pair is particularly relevant to Plato's *Republic,* with its concern for the education and manner of life of the ruling class. The Roman pair gives us a historical illustration of the primary struggle which actuates political life according to Aristotle, namely, that between the democratic and the oligarchical parties in the state. Since Greece at the time described by Plutarch was already becoming a second-rate power, let us concentrate on the Roman events, which occur near the height of the Roman republic's military power, and perhaps even mark the beginning of its decline.

By the time Tiberius and Caius Gracchus reached manhood, Rome had fought and won the third and last of the Punic Wars. The first Punic War had started in 265 B.C. and the third one ended, with the total destruction and razing of Carthage, in 146 B.C. These wars definitely established Rome as the major power in the Mediterranean Sea. Its supremacy in Italy was never again questioned, and the war had forced Rome to become a major sea power in order to cope with Carthage. Rome became master of the islands of Sardinia, Corsica, and Sicily; Spain and Africa were added as colonies to the Roman possessions.

The Punic Wars are indelibly connected, on the Roman side, with the name of Scipio (just as they are, on the Carthaginian side, with the name of Hannibal). The Gracchi are doubly related to the Scipios, four generations of whom were involved in the last two Punic Wars. Two of the Scipios so distinguished themselves for their generalship in these wars that they were surnamed "Africanus." The first Publius Cornelius Scipio and his brother Gnaeus both fought in Spain and Gaul against the Carthaginians; they were slain in the same battle. The son of Cornelius, also named Publius Cornelius Scipio, rose to command and fame shortly after the disastrous defeat which Hannibal inflicted on the Roman forces at Cannae. He, too, fought in Spain; then he carried the war into Africa itself and defeated Hannibal decisively at Zama. This earned him the name of Africanus. His daughter, Cornelia, was the mother of the Gracchi. His son (again named Publius Cornelius Scipio) adopted the son of L. Aemilius Paulus, the conqueror of Macedonia and himself the son of the Roman consul who was defeated by Hannibal at Cannae. This adopted son—called Publius Cornelius Scipio Aemilianus—was thus the grandson of the victim of Hannibal as well as the adopted grandson of Hannibal's conqueror. He was a Roman general in the Third Punic War, conquering and destroying Carthage; this earned him, too, the surname "Africanus." This younger Africanus married Sempronia, the sister of the Gracchi. The Gracchi, therefore, were grandsons of Scipio Africanus the elder, and brothers-in-law of Scipio Africanus the younger.

Thus the Gracchi were members of a noble and distinguished patrician family. Yet their political careers were spent almost entirely in opposition to the Senate. This is understandable when we realize that in the second century B.C. Rome was no longer an aristocracy, nor was the Senate the truly ruling power in it. Though the old forms were preserved, the govern-

GENEALOGY OF THE GRACCHI

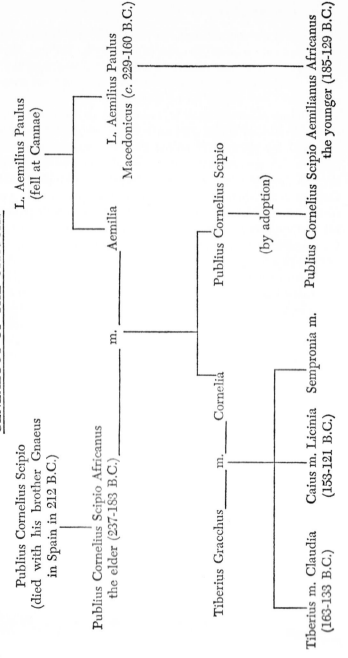

ment was really an oligarchy. Fitting perfectly into Aristotle's description, Rome was ruled by a few wealthy families. Rome had had, after the expulsion of its kings, a republican form of government, in which a small patrician class was the ruling aristocracy. The Senate was composed of the patricians, and two consuls were chosen from the patricians every year. But gradually, the common people (the plebs) managed to achieve more and more power, principally through the institution of the tribunes. It is difficult to say what the office of the tribune consisted in. Initially the tribunes were supposed to protect the people from excesses of the ruling class; later on, they also proposed legislation as the assembly of the people became more and more powerful and the Senate less and less so.

But the changes that took place were more than a mere shifting of power from the aristocrats to the people. In fact, at the time of the Gracchi, neither Senate nor plebs ruled. There had sprung up instead a new ruling class: the rich landholders. The Senate's power became diminished through the tribunate as well as through the establishment of a law that enabled plebeians to become consuls. The people, on the other hand, could not grasp the power that was slipping from the Senate. This was due, in part, to the fact that the arrangement of offices (*i.e.*, what Aristotle calls the constitution) favored rule by a small number; in part it was due to the continuing wars of the third and second centuries B.C. These wars ruined the Roman middle class; *i.e.*, the small landholders. Instead of working their land, they became soldiers; and though service in the legions had originally been considered an honor and privilege, it soon became necessary to reward soldiers and veterans with pay. While the majority of Roman citizens were, therefore, serving in the legions and probably even preferred it to the hard work on their farms, a few wealthy men were buying up the land and slaves, who were being brought into Rome in great numbers as a result of its successful wars.

The Gracchi proposed agrarian reforms to stem the growing tide of landless, homeless, and rootless ex-soldiers. Since they used as their public forum the office of the tribunate, and since the Senate quickly lined up against them, the struggle had the appearance of being between the people and the Senate. It was really, however, between the people who were many and poor, and the few who were rich and who held land.

Let us glance at the events that followed the appearance of the Gracchi on the Roman scene, to see how one kind of government followed another. From an aristocracy, Rome passed to an oligarchy. The oligarchy aroused the ire of the people, and, in the ensuing struggle, the popular party reached such strength for a short time that civil war resulted. Very quickly, then, tyrannical excesses sprang up in the reigns of Marius and Sulla, and finally Rome's government passed to the emperors—at best, benevolent despots, at worst, tyrants.

II

Plutarch is not wrong in thinking that there is much similarity between the Greek and the Roman men and events. In the life of Agis, he reports that a certain Epitadeus

proposed a decree that all men should have liberty to dispose of their land by gift in their lifetime, or by their last will and testament.

This . . . was the ruin of the best state of the commonwealth. For the rich men without scruple drew the estate into their own hands, excluding the rightful heirs from their succession; and all the wealth being centred upon the few, the generality were poor and miserable. Honourable pursuits, for which there was no longer leisure, were neglected; the state was filled with sordid business, and with hatred and envy of the rich. There did not remain above seven hundred of the old Spartan families, of which, perhaps, one hundred might have estates in land; the rest were destitute alike of wealth and of honour, were tardy and unperforming in the defence of their country against its enemies abroad, and eagerly watched the opportunity for change and revolution at home. (p. 650b-c)

Here Plutarch reports exactly the same situation as that which we saw in Rome: an oligarchy developing because the wealth of the country is being concentrated in a few hands. And Agis' proposals are just like those of the Gracchi: cancellation of debts and redistribution of the land.

This illustrates a point that Aristotle makes in the *Politics*: although the literal meaning of oligarchy is "rule of the few" and that of democracy is "rule of the many," the real difference between democracy and oligarchy is poverty and wealth. Wherever men rule by reason of their wealth, whether they be few or many, that is an oligarchy, and where the poor rule, that is a democracy. But as a fact the rich are few and the poor many . . . (*Politics,* Book III, Ch. 8, Vol. 9, p. 477b-c)

The subject of wealth comes up again in the life of Cleomenes, when Cleomenes defends his use of violence by declaring that

if it had been possible for him without bloodshed to free Lacedaemon from those foreign plagues, luxury, sumptuosity, debts, and usury, and from those yet more ancient evils, poverty and riches, he should have thought himself the happiest king . . . (p. 660c)

Then Cleomenes tells the nation

the whole land was now their common property; debtors should be cleared of their debts . . . (p. 660d)

A little later Plutarch adds that Cleomenes

began to consult about the education of the youth, and the discipline, as they call it; . . . and in a short time the schools of exercise and the common tables recovered their ancient decency and order, a few out of necessity, but the most voluntarily, returning to that generous and Laconic way of living. (pp. 660d-661a)

It is quite evident from these four lives that all four men (and Plutarch also) are convinced that economic inequalities are the basic reason for weakness in the state, and that economic injustice must be remedied by political means. The great importance which they all ascribe to having a middle class of small landowners—constituting the bulk of the *citizens*—is an indication of how appropriate it was for Aristotle to treat of economics in the first book of the *Politics*. The citizen, in order to handle properly his office of citizenship, must have and be able to manage some property of his own. This appears to be Aristotle's view, on theoretical grounds; but evidently Agis, Cleomenes, Tiberius and Caius Gracchus all agree, on very practical grounds. Nevertheless, it will be useful to examine this conception of citizenship, and to ask some questions also about the means employed by these men to achieve this kind of citizenry.

III

*Is the view that the citizen must be a propertied man
to be accepted without further qualification?*

Some qualifications certainly seem to be in order. We must
remember that the purpose of these four "agrarian reformers"
(as we may style them) was to increase the number of citizens
who could truly discharge their office. The evil which all four
were combating was the concentration of wealth in just a few
hands. Therefore, they were as much opposed to the demand
for a high property qualification (which would eliminate all but
a handful of very rich men from the rolls of citizenship) as they
were opposed to propertyless men exercising the functions of
citizens. Indeed, it could be said that rather than seeking to
make ownership of property a prerequisite for citizenship, they
looked upon property as the due of citizens or their reward.

*Would ownership of property by itself make men
good citizens?*

The question is obviously rhetorical; yet there clearly is some
connection between property and citizenship. But what is it?
And, to return to the paragraph above, *which is the requirement for which?* Furthermore, is not all this concern with land
and property perhaps a little excessive? Granted that a large
citizenry of small property holders would be less subject to
pressures and abuses than an impoverished proletariat, it is
clear that there can be bad citizens even in such a state. At best,
property can be a condition which tends toward a better citizenry. It may help to secure the dignity and independence of
free men.

*Is the ownership of property connected with citizen-
ship in the same way under all kinds of constitutions? Or is it intimately connected only with the
oligarchical form of government?*

Offhand, one would be tempted to take the second alternative; yet the odd thing is that Agis, Cleomenes, and the Grac-

chi were all *opposing* the oligarchs. They were using their property demands as a means of democratizing the constitution. That seems strange. For if we consider the names of the various kinds of constitutions, we find that monarchy gives the rule to *one,* democracy to *many,* aristocracy to the *best,* oligarchy to the *few.* Aristotle corrects this by saying that in an oligarchy political power is in the hands of the *rich* who are the *few.* In his analysis, property ownership would be a requirement only in an oligarchy. He does not mention property in connection with tyranny and polity, the remaining two forms of government.

What is the twist whereby an apparently oligarchical measure—the association of citizenship with property—becomes an antioligarchical and prodemocratic maneuver?

Probably, all depends on the situation that exists when the maneuver takes place. If many citizens already own property and they are required to possess more property than most of them have to qualify for citizenship, then such a move would be oligarchical. If, on the other hand, a few citizens own most of the wealth, then a move to diffuse ownership and property would be democratic in character.

Were the demands of these reformers just?

The last paragraph necessarily raises this question. For what makes the reformers' plans democratic is that they proposed to take away property from the very rich and give it to the poor. Now this may have been a very worthy end, and good for the state, but does it accord with the just rights of the rich? Is what these men proposed and executed not expropriation? Is employing such a means justified by their end (assuming that their end is just and that their end would be furthered by these means)?

Can we defend these reformers against the charge of rabble-rousing?

Were they not at least demagogues, since all their legislative proposals were designed to favor the people? And although all four of them seem to have been upright and virtuous men, could not the precedent which they set be considered dangerous? For instance, although these reforms may have been motivated by a desire to further the common good, the people may have misunderstood this and assumed that they were being bribed by men who desired political power.

Is interference in economic affairs ever a proper political matter?

Evidently there was much more of such interference in ancient times than we now tolerate. Plato envisaged very stringent sumptuary laws in the *Republic*, and Sparta actually had them. Of course, the eighteenth amendment to the United States Constitution prohibiting alcoholic liquor was something of the same sort. And it is often claimed that the modern tax structure not only raises revenue, but actually is an instrument of economic policy that affects the distribution of wealth. The United States seems opposed to government expropriation of land or other property, though law recognizes the right of eminent domain. Great Britain, however, after World War II "nationalized" certain businesses (like railways and coal). And there is some precedent in the United States for the distribution (if not the taking away) of land, in the Homesteading Acts that gave public lands to those who worked them.

The following questions are designed to help you test the thoroughness of your reading. Each question is to be answered by giving a page or pages of the reading assignment. Answers will be found on page 219 of this Reading Plan.

1 What were the details of Agis' law?

2 Did this law pass?

3 What was Agesilaus' proposal, by which he frustrated Agis' design?

4 Was there any family connection between Agis and Cleomenes?

5 Describe Cleomenes' manner of holding court as king.

6 Give Cleomenes' arguments against suicide.

7 How did Tiberius Gracchus overcome the tribune Octavius' objections to his (Tiberius') land reform bill?

8 How did Tiberius defend his deposition of a tribune (i.e., of Octavius)?

9 What was the inscription on the statue of Cornelia?

10 What changes did Caius Gracchus make in the courts of justice?

11 Why was Caius not elected tribune for a third time ?

12 How did Caius die?

OLD TESTAMENT

I Samuel, (D) I Kings

NEW TESTAMENT

Matthew, 22:15–22

Acts, 21:1–26:32

The Western tradition is heir to Judaeo-Christian as well as to Greco-Roman thought. The Bible is an important source for our basic political ideas.

Most of us remember the moving story of a people brought together out of nomadic tribes and united in a covenant with the God of righteousness and justice who is the ruler of all things. But we may forget that in ancient Israel there was no separation of the religious and the secular life. This fact underlies the political significance of the biblical selections with which we are here concerned.

The selection from the Old Testament deals with the problem of how a people which has agreed to be ruled by God can appoint a human king. Is there a basic tension between religious and political loyalties? The passage from Matthew deals with the problem of conforming to the administrative requirements of a pagan empire. Whom shall we serve, God or Caesar? And the third text, from the Acts of the Apostles, shows how the Roman concept of citizenship conflicts with the demands of religious orthodoxy.

The biblical questions and answers differ from those in Greco-Roman political thought. For the latter, the problem of the form of government concerns the alternatives of monarchy, aristocracy, and democracy. In the Bible, it concerns the choice between God and man, between divine and human law. The question is not one of freedom or slavery in the civil sense, but adherence or nonadherence to the rule of God. This concern played a part in Western political thought down to fairly recent times. Early settlers in New England were imbued with the biblical ideas of "theocracy."

Fourth Reading

I

This assignment consists of biblical texts relevant to politics and government. We are dealing with the Bible here as a historical document, not as sacred scripture. For the purpose of this guide we are concerned with the Jewish people's attitude toward statecraft at various times in their history.

We have selected unconnected passages from three different books of the Bible as our basic texts. This is necessary, because there is no single biblical book dealing with politics. The historical books of the Old Testament present a detailed chronicle of events in ancient Israel. But the passages we have selected give some of the essential biblical ideas on politics in an incisive form.

II

Our first text is from the first book of Samuel (or Kings, in the Douay version). It records the transition from theocracy to monarchy in the government of Israel. In the days of the patriarchs Abraham, Isaac, and Jacob there was no government, except for the rule of the father over the family or clan. When, however, the descendants of Jacob, or Israel, fled from Egypt, they had increased sufficiently to require some sort of centralized leadership. Their leader was Moses, who bore no specific political title.

The Jewish people regarded themselves as being governed by God Himself. They ascribed the moral and ceremonial regulations handed down by Moses as coming from God. The word *Torah*, usually translated "Law," actually means "teaching," "guidance," or "word." This word is addressed to the people through their leader. Thus Leviticus begins as follows:

And the Lord called unto Moses, and spake unto him out of the taber-
nacle of the congregation, saying,

Speak unto the children of Israel, and say unto them, If any man of you
bring an offering unto the Lord, ye shall bring your offering of the
cattle . . . (Leviticus, 1:1-2)

There follows then a set of rules and regulations concerning sacrificial offerings to God. Although Moses announces the
law to the children of Israel, he is not the lawmaker. He is a
"prophet," literally a spokesman for God. He merely transmits
what God says. God is the Lord or King of Israel. He makes
the law and punishes transgressors. He also tells the children of
Israel through his spokesmen how to conduct their "foreign
policy," *i.e.*, He tells them where to settle, which peoples they
should fight, and so on. This is theocracy, a government headed
by God. It rests on a covenant between God and His people.

In Deuteronomy, 17:14-20, there is a prophecy that some-
day Israel will have kings:

When thou art come unto the land which the Lord thy God giveth thee,
and shalt possess it, and shalt dwell therein, and shalt say, I will set a
king over me, like as all the nations that are about me;

Thou shalt in any wise set him king over thee, whom the Lord thy
God shall choose: one from among thy brethren shalt thou set king over
thee: thou mayest not set a stranger over thee, which is not thy brother.
(Deuteronomy, 17:14-15)

This passage shows that it was unusual in that time and place
not to have a king.

After the deaths of Moses and Joshua, this loose-knit con-
federation was led by a succession of "judges," or military cham-
pions (Gideon, Samson, Deborah). These judges ascribed their
power and appointment to God and did not claim the preroga-
tive of passing on their divine calling to heirs or disciples.

Then the men of Israel said unto Gideon, Rule thou over us, both thou,
and thy son, and thy son's son also: for thou hast delivered us from the
hand of Midian.

And Gideon said unto them, I will not rule over you, neither shall my
son rule over you: the Lord shall rule over you. (Judges, 8:22-23)

The book of Judges refers many times to the fact that there

was no king in Israel (see Judges, 17:6, 18:1, 19:1, 21:25, (D) 17:6, 18:1, 18:31, 21:24). Twice we hear the refrain:

In those days there was no king in Israel, but every man did that which was right in his own eyes. (Judges, 17:6, 21:25, (D) 17:6, 21:24)

Many interpretations of this text are possible. It may be a nostalgic reference to a time when there was no strong central government and only a loose familial or tribal rule prevailed. Or it may be a condemnation of anarchy in politics and religion. A similar text in Deuteronomy (12:8) refers to a time before worship had a formal and organized pattern. In any event such passages indicate a time when no formal political authority governed Israel.

But how could a people permanently committed to rule by God choose a human ruler? How could Israel dare to ask for a king to govern them? Would this not be blasphemy? Would not God be angry at Israel? Our next text is quite emphatic about this:

But the thing displeased Samuel, when they said, Give us a king to judge us. And Samuel prayed unto the Lord.

And the Lord said unto Samuel, Hearken unto the voice of the people in all that they say unto thee: for they have not rejected thee, but they have rejected me, that I should not reign over them. (I Samuel, 8:6-7, (D) I Kings, 8:6-7)

Samuel warns the Israelites of all the iniquities they will have to endure from a tyrannical king, but this is to no avail:

Nevertheless the people refused to obey the voice of Samuel; and they said, Nay; but we will have a king over us;

That we also may be like all the nations; and that our king may judge us, and go out before us, and fight our battles. (I Samuel, 8:19-20, (D) I Kings, 8:19-20)

There is, however, an ambiguity in the first book of Samuel on this whole question of theocracy versus monarchy. On the one hand, Israel is condemned for wanting a king and thus rejecting God. On the other hand, God Himself points out Saul as the man who is to be king. In Chapter 10 His prophet-priest Samuel anoints Saul, and says, "The Lord hath anointed thee to be captain over his inheritance." He tells Saul that God will inspire him, that God is with him. Saul prophesies and is accompanied by men "touched" by God. Thus it is clear that, although it may have been wrong for Israel to set up a kingdom, God is still at the helm. He picks out the man who is to be king, and that man is divinely inspired, with prophetic powers.

III

The second part of the reading assignment revolves around Christ's pronouncement, "Render unto Caesar the things which are Caesar's; and unto God the things that are God's" (Matthew, 22:15-22). The same story of Christ's encounter with the Pharisees occurs also in Mark, 12:13-17 and in Luke, 20:21-26.

A provocative question is asked: "Is it lawful to give tribute unto Caesar, or not?" Can a good Jew, with his heart set on the Kingdom of God, bow down before a pagan emperor? A negative answer would be seditious. A positive answer might betray impiety or inconsistency. But Jesus chooses neither the path of rebellion nor the way of conformity. He picks up a coin, points to Caesar's image on it, and says that this kind of thing belongs to the imperial rulers. The things of spirit and truth belong to God. Jesus divides the political and the religious realm. Render unto each its own, He says.

IV

The third part of the reading assignment is taken from the Acts of the Apostles. This book of the Bible is no more a political treatise than the others we have read. It is sacred history, bearing witness to the origin of the Christian Church and the major events of its early years. Much of the book deals with the missionary journeys of the apostle Paul and what befell him. This account is of interest here because it shows the workings of the Roman judicial system. Judaea was a Roman province, ruled either by Roman procurators or by kings appointed by Rome. In this portion of the Acts, two procurators are mentioned by name, Felix and Porcius Festus; there is also reference to the Jewish king, Agrippa. They are involved in the judicial procedures having to do with Paul.

Let us glance at the incidents that brought Paul into contact with Roman law and justice. A mob was stirred up against Paul in Jerusalem. They thought that Paul had been teaching sacrilegious doctrines, and tried to kill him. A Roman captain and his soldiers stopped the lynching and took Paul into custody (Chapter 21).

Paul addressed the mob and told them of his conversion and his becoming an apostle to the Gentiles. The crowd grew so violent at this that the perplexed captain ordered Paul flogged to get information out of him. But when Paul told the captain that he was a Roman citizen, the captain countermanded his order. We see that Roman citizenship was a valuable privilege, for a Roman citizen could not be flogged without due process of law. When Paul's appearance before the high Jewish council again resulted in an uproar, the captain considered it his duty to protect Paul:

And when there arose a great dissension, the chief captain, fearing lest Paul should have been pulled in pieces of them, commanded the soldiers to go down, and to take him by force from among them, and to bring him into the castle. (Acts, 23:10)

After this, when some Jews plotted to kill Paul, the captain decided to send Paul to Caesarea (the city from which Judaea was governed) to the governor, Felix. Again, it was Paul's Roman citizenship that made the captain so concerned about him, for he wrote to the governor:

This man was taken of the Jews, and should have been killed of them: then came I with an army, and rescued him, having understood that he was a Roman. (23:27)

Paul's alleged transgressions were next argued before Felix, who, however, deferred judgment, apparently for two years (see 24:27). Meanwhile Paul was guarded by a centurion, but otherwise seems to have suffered no hardship. When Felix was succeeded by Porcius Festus, it became Festus' duty to dispose of the case.

Festus was ready to turn Paul over to the Jewish authorities at Jerusalem, thinking that this was an internal Jewish matter. But Paul refused to go to Jerusalem and instead invoked the privilege of a Roman citizen to appeal to Caesar himself. Festus, of course, had to grant this request and he prepared to send Paul to Rome, there to be judged by Caesar himself. But he declared himself to be a little puzzled as to just what Paul was accused of. Accordingly, he asked King Agrippa, a Jew, to examine Paul, in order to find out just what the disagreement between Paul and the Jews was. From the point of view of judicial procedure, it is interesting to note the following words of Festus:

> It is not the manner of the Romans to deliver any man to die, before that he which is accused have the accusers face to face, and have licence to answer for himself concerning the crime laid against him. (25:16)

The examination by Agrippa turned mainly on the question of Christ's Resurrection. Both Agrippa and Festus were impressed with Paul; we read that Agrippa said, "Almost thou persuadest me to be a Christian," while Festus uttered the famous words, "Paul, thou art beside thyself; much learning doth make thee mad." King and governor agreed that Paul did not seem to have committed any crime deserving of death or imprisonment. However, the matter had gone too far. Since Paul had appealed to Caesar he must be sent to Rome. Nobody else could now judge his case.

V

Is theocracy a form of government comparable with other forms?

This question might also be phrased this way: Is there really such a form of government as theocracy? Or are there really only various forms of government, such as monarchy, aristocracy, and democracy, each of which may claim to be led by God? The history of the Jewish people as it is recorded in the five books of Moses, and in Joshua, Judges, Samuel, Kings, and Chronicles, illustrates the difficulty of isolating theocracy as a pure form of government.

Did God rule the Israelites directly in their exodus from Egypt and their wanderings through the desert? If so, what was Moses' role? Presumably he was God's vicegerent, that is, he acted in God's place. Similarly, Joshua and the judges that succeeded him were vicegerents of God. But how does vicegerency differ from kingship? This question is especially difficult to answer, when the king is chosen by God Himself and is anointed by God's priest, as was the case with Saul. Nevertheless, we may be able to detect a slight difference. Even though it is slight, it can have tremendous practical importance.

The vicegerent of God acts *for* God; he acts in God's place, though on rare occasions God Himself directly intervenes in the affairs of His people. An edict pronounced by God's vicegerent is, therefore, an edict of God. Indeed, throughout the five books of Moses, it is made clear that the so-called Mosaic law is really God's law. Though the various edicts are not laid down by God speaking directly to the people, God does speak directly to Moses and commands him to announce the law to the people.

For instance, Leviticus, 17 begins: "And the Lord spake unto Moses, saying, Speak unto Aaron, and unto his sons, and unto all the children of Israel, and say unto them; . . ." And Chapter 18 begins: "And the Lord spake unto Moses, saying, Speak unto the children of Israel, and say unto them, . . ." Similarly, in Chapters 19, 20, 21, etc.

Since God's vicegerent speaks for God, there is no appeal from his word. To whom could such an appeal be directed? Of course, the vicegerent may fail in his duty, since he is merely human. But in such a case he will be punished by God. Thus we are told in Numbers, 20:7-13 that Moses doubted God; and accordingly God punishes him by not letting him come into Canaan.

The position of king is more ambiguous. On the one hand, he, too, is a kind of vicegerent, and God acts through him. We saw in the case of Saul that God picked the king and filled him with His spirit. The king is the anointed (Messiah) of God, and his person is inviolate, touched by a divine aura. He often assumes a priestlike role in worship. On the other hand, he can be held accountable by God and His prophets as well as by the people for his ethical and religious failings. Military disasters and famines are considered as God's punishment for the king's wickedness. Remember Elijah's ferocious invective against Ahab, Nathan pointing the finger at David, and the popular revolutions against royal houses. Such opposition and temerity from commoners is unique in the kingdoms of the ancient Middle East.

Clearly kings had more formal stature and autonomy than judges. They dealt with the day-to-day details of legislation and policy themselves. They were tinged with divinity, but under divine law themselves and personally responsible for their actions. Some thinkers have seen Israel's kingship as resting on an original covenant between the people and the king, before God.

What are the things that are Caesar's, and what the things that are God's?

This is, of course, the important question with respect to Christ's remark. It is easy to agree with the exhortation; for instance, it seems to meet the demands of justice: render to each his due. But the difficulty is in knowing what is due to God and what is due to secular rulers.

In modern terms, we might say that this remark urges the separation of church and state. "Give to the state what is due to the state, and give to the church what is due to the church." Here it is important to note that the separation of church and state was unthinkable in Israel before the Babylonian exile. Only after the kingdom had been destroyed, and the nation lay under foreign rule did a separate church emerge. Israel the religious community survived Israel the national state. In a theocracy church and state are one. In Israel, even under the monarchy, the sacred and secular spheres were hard to separate. Jewish kings performed the sacrifices and other rites of the religion. The separation of priesthood and kingship is a product of later Judaism. It is, of course, absolutely necessary for a universal faith like Christianity. But here, too, priests assumed temporal powers and princes assumed priestly roles.

This still does not answer our orginal question: Which functions belong to the state and which to the church?

Is education the business of the state or of the church? Can this question be answered by dividing education into purely intellectual training and moral training? Is moral training the business of the church alone? Or does it belong to the state alone? Or to both? Or does it belong to neither, but instead to the family?

Are contractual matters the concern of the state? Is there any difficulty about the institution of marriage? Is it a contract? Is it also the business of the church? To what extent?

Can there be a conflict between the commands of the state and those of religion? In such a case, which should prevail? Who decides? Can a man appeal to church, God, or religion to avoid obeying what he considers an unjust law? (Consider the case of conscientious objectors.)

Must the state respect all religious practices, no matter how offensive they may be to established customs? (Consider the case of polygamy and the Mormon religion.) Must the church tolerate all secular laws, no matter how immoral and unjust they may be? (Consider the case of the churches in Germany during the Nazi regime.)

What are the rights and duties of citizenship especially with respect to religion?

From the Acts it is quite clear that Roman citizenship was a great privilege. What was important to Paul was that he did not have to be tried by the authorities in the provinces; he could and did demand that he be tried in Rome before Caesar.

The right to try crimes committed within its own boundaries is a right that any sovereign country guards jealously; it is one of the surest signs of effective sovereignty. The fact that the province of Judaea (or any other Roman province) did not have it shows both how thoroughly subdued the provinces were and how valuable Roman citizenship was. By contrast, we must remember that, for instance, United States citizens traveling in

European countries are subject to the laws of those countries. This, of course, does not show that United States citizenship is any less valuable than Roman citizenship was, but rather that countries like Great Britain, France, Italy, etc., are also sovereign.

Let us turn more particularly to the rights and duties of citizenship as far as religion is concerned. These rights and duties have, of course, varied greatly from time to time and place to place. It is clear also that religion can have no rights *against* the state at all, unless church and state are separate. In a theocracy, a citizen can plead no religious rights against the state. An offense against the state is an offense against religion, and similarly a religious offense is also a secular offense. In other words, religious tolerance is not possible in a theocracy.

But even in other forms of government, religious tolerance is not possible (*i.e.*, the citizen can have no right to oppose the state on religious matters) unless there is true separation of church and state. As long as there is a state religion, for example, there are certain duties of religious observance that are incumbent upon the citizen. There may be a high degree of near tolerance in such a state, however. For instance, we learn from Gibbon (see Chapter 16 of the *Decline and Fall of the Roman Empire* in Vol. 40) that the various religions of the empire were tolerated as long as their adherents were willing to participate in certain merely formal rites of the state religion, (the worship of the Caesars who were considered divine). It was the Christians' unwillingness to consent to even such formalities that led eventually to their persecution.

In the Constitution of the United States, the first amendment deals with religion: "Congress shall make no law respecting an establishment of religion, or prohibiting the free exercise thereof . . ."

The problems of religious tolerance are complex. We often hear that rights and duties go together. Does a citizen only have the right to freedom of religious belief and worship or are there also certain duties connected with this? Does the state have any rights against the churches? Does the separation of church and state imply not only that there is no established religion, but also that secularism is officially advocated by the state? Or is secularism as much a religion as any of the particular faiths? Is it consistent with the doctrine of separation of church and state to include in the oath of allegiance to the United States the phrase "under God"? Does this take away religious freedom from citizens who do not believe in God?

The following questions are designed to help you test the thoroughness of your reading. Each question is to be answered by giving a chapter and verse (or verses) from the reading assignment. Answers will be found on page 219 of this Reading Plan.

1 What was the transgression of Jonathan for which his father Saul wanted to put him to death?

2 What is the difference with respect to resurrection in the opinion of the Pharisees and the Sadducees?

3 Where was Paul born?

4 Why does the Lord reject Saul from being king?

5 What is the accusation that the high priest and the Jews bring against Paul?

6 What made Saul jealous of David?

7 Why did David play the harp for Saul?

8 How did Saul die?

TACITUS

The Annals

Books I, XIII–XVI

Vol. 15, pp. 1–23, 125–184

Sometimes we have to get our history from writers with humdrum minds who express themselves in a dull and deadly style which embalms rather than recreates the events and persons of the past. But history comes alive when we learn it from Publius Cornelius Tacitus, eminent lawyer, senator, and consul, who lived under nine Caesars and who recounts for us the events of his days and years.

This is no dispassionate report by a detached spectator. Tacitus writes out of intense political and ethical convictions. He holds up to our gaze the corruption and iniquity which he finds inherent in the new imperial rule, and measures it against the virtue and integrity of the old patrician and republican order.

The annals of imperial Rome come from the pen of one of the greatest prose writers in Western literature. His character sketches are masterpieces of incisive portrayal. His recital of the terrible events of the time is dramatically staged. How memorable is the account of the murder of Agrippina, Nero's mother! As Nero's henchmen close in to dispatch her, she is finally convinced that her own son intends her death. "Smite my womb," she says, presenting her body to the assassin's sword, and naming the author of her tragic end.

Tacitus is famous for his brevity. His characterizations are achieved with a minimum of detail. He can sum up complex historical situations in a few words. Thus, for example, he reveals how the Roman conquerors of Britain looked to the British by having a British chieftain say: "They make a wilderness, and call it peace." Tacitus used only four words in the original Latin.

Fifth Reading

I

Remarkably little is known concerning the personal life of Tacitus. The dates of his birth and death are matters of conjecture, and there is even some doubt whether his full name was Publius Cornelius Tacitus or Gaius Cornelius Tacitus. Such information concerning him as we do have comes from only two sources: allusions to himself in his own works, and eleven letters addressed to him by his friend Pliny the Younger.

Pliny speaks of himself and Tacitus as being "much of an age"; probably, however, Tacitus was slightly older. Pliny was born in either A.D. 61 or 62, and hence it is usually inferred that Tacitus was born in the year A.D. 55. It is thought that he died sometime around A.D. 117. Thus his life span encompassed the reigns of the emperors Nero, Galba, Otho, Vitellius, Vespasian, Titus, Domitian, Nerva, and Trajan. He himself has this to say about himself and about his work at the beginning of the *Histories:*

I myself knew nothing of Galba, of Otho, or of Vitellius, either from benefits or from injuries. I would not deny that my elevation was begun by Vespasian, augmented by Titus, and still further advanced by Domitian; but those who profess inviolable truthfulness must speak of all without partiality and without hatred. I have reserved as an employment for my old age, should my life be long enough, a subject at once more fruitful and less anxious in the reign of the Divine Nerva and the empire of Trajan, enjoying the rare happiness of times, when we may think what we please, and express what we think. (p. 189b)

Tacitus himself escaped the wrath of Domitian, even under the reign of terror during Domitian's last three years, and was, as he says, in fact further advanced by him. Nevertheless, he looked with melancholy on the servile state of Rome and its citizens, which reached its height under Domitian. In the early part of his *Life of Agricola* (probably written in A.D. 98) he describes his repugnance for the state of Rome under Domitian:

As a former age had witnessed the extreme of liberty, so we witnessed the extreme of servitude, when the informer robbed us of the interchange of speech and hearing. We should have lost memory as well as voice, had it been as easy to forget as to keep silence.

And near the end of the same work, he compares the villainy of Nero and Domitian:

Even Nero turned his eyes away, and did not gaze upon the atrocities which he ordered; with Domitian it was the chief part of our miseries to see and to be seen, to know that our sighs were being recorded, to have, ever ready to note the pallid looks of so many faces, that savage countenance reddened with the hue with which he defied shame.

There is little doubt that although the *Histories* and *Annals* were composed in happy times, the experience of living under Domitian left a lasting mark on Tacitus. All his descriptions of the events at Rome that have come down to us are infected with the melancholy and sadness of one who has himself seen incredible acts of tyranny, degradation, and folly.

II

The *Histories* originally contained twelve books, while the *Annals* comprised eighteen books. What we now have of them are, therefore, large fragments. In the *Annals* Books V, VI, XI, and XVI are fragmentary, while Books VII-X and XVII-XVIII are missing entirely. The missing portions include the entire reign of Caius Caesar (Caligula), the first six years of Claudius' reign and the last three years of Nero's reign. In the *Histories* only the first four books and a fragment of the fifth have survived, and thus Tacitus' treatment of the reigns of Vespasian, Titus, and Domitian is lost to us.

Our reading assignment consists of the first book of the *Annals*, which records the beginning of the reign of Tiberius, the immediate successor of Augustus. We then skip to Books XIII-XVI, which describe the reign of Nero. Book XVI, which deals with the last years of Nero's life and reign, is incomplete as we have it. Here is the rest of the story:

In the autumn of 65 Nero's wife Poppaea died. There was pestilence in Rome. Early in the summer of 66 the Parthian prince Tiridates came to Rome to receive the crown of Armenia at Nero's hands. This event had been agreed upon in a conference between Corbulo and Tiridates, as Tacitus tells us in Book XV, Chapter 29 (p. 164d). In the fall of 66 Nero visited Greece and was both spectator of and participant in the great Greek festivals of art. While he was gone, rebellion broke out, first in Gaul and then in Germany. Nero returned, but found both populace and Senate hostile. The governor of Hispania Tarraconensis, Galba, claimed the throne. The Senate soon proclaimed Galba as emperor and passed sentence of death on Nero. Nero met his fate in the traditional Roman way. He committed suicide on June 9, 68, at the age of 31 and in the fourteenth year of his reign. With him ended the line of emperors descended from Julius Caesar.

III

In the portion of the *Annals* that we read there seems to be an approximately equal division between Tacitus' description of events at Rome and events abroad. But we sense that the domestic scene is of more interest to Tacitus than the foreign. We may call Tacitus a political historian; that is, a historian who primarily recorded political events rather than external affairs. As such a historian, he is above all a moralist. Like his contemporary Plutarch, Tacitus grieves at the loss of the ancient Roman liberty and the old republican virtues. He begins the *Annals* thus:

Rome at the beginning was ruled by kings. Freedom and the consulship were established by Lucius Brutus.

In the second sentence, therefore, he associates freedom with consulship, or the republican form of government. But by the time of the emperor Augustus, according to Tacitus, Roman freedom and virtue were no more:

The State had been revolutionised, and there was not a vestige left of the old sound morality. Stript of equality, all looked up to the commands of a sovereign without the least apprehension for the present, while Augustus in the vigour of life, could maintain his own position, that of his house, and the general tranquillity. (p. 2a)

We may wonder whether Tacitus' experiences with Domitian did not make him unable or unwilling to see anything good in the entire line of emperors, and the events at Rome, prior to Nerva and Trajan. To be sure, he states his purpose in writing the *Annals* as follows:

My purpose is to relate a few facts about Augustus—more particularly his last acts, then the reign of Tiberius, and all which follows, without either bitterness or partiality, from any motives to which I am far removed. (p. 1a-b)

But his impartiality seems rather dubious when we read later on in Book I (Chapter 52) a passage like this:

The news [of Germanicus's victory] was a source of joy and also of anxiety to Tiberius. He rejoiced that the mutiny was crushed, but the fact that Germanicus had won the soldiers' favour by lavishing money, and promptly granting the discharge, as well as his fame as a soldier, annoyed him. Still, he brought his achievements under the notice of the Senate, and spoke much of his greatness in language elaborated for effect, more so than could be believed to come from his inmost heart. (p. 15c-d)

The facts, as Tacitus records them, indicate that Tiberius praised Germanicus; but the historian somehow distrusts the motives of Tiberius, so much so that the fullness of the praise is only an indication to him of the emperor's hypocrisy, it being "more so than could be believed to come from his inmost heart."

But while Tacitus' gloom over the end of the Roman republic may have caused him to overlook some of the virtues of Augustus and Tiberius, there is little doubt that his evident loathing for the emperor Nero was only too well founded. Nero's capacity for revenge and murder apparently knew no bounds. He killed his brother Britannicus, his mother Agrippina, and his wife Octavia. He likewise killed (or caused to commit suicide) his teacher and adviser Seneca, the Stoic philosopher, as well as vast numbers of other Roman senators, nobles, and officeholders.

Yet none of these events was able to stir the Romans from their attitude of servility and flattery. Thus Tacitus remarks after the death of Octavia:

And for all this offerings were voted to the temples. I record the fact with a special object. Whoever would study the calamities of that period in my pages or those of other authors, is to take it for granted that as often as the emperor directed banishments or executions, so often was there a thanksgiving to the gods, and what formerly commemorated some prosperous event, was then a token of public disaster. Still, if any decree of the Senate was marked by some new flattery, or by the lowest servility, I shall not pass it over in silence. (p. 157c)

Just as instructive concerning the moral and intellectual climate at Rome is Tacitus' account of Seneca's downfall. Here there is no comment by the author; he simply sets down what happened in such a concise way that the corruption that existed in Rome becomes terrifyingly clear.

Seneca was assailed by slanderers after the death of Burrus; the two of them had been the chief advisers of Nero when he ascended to the throne. When Seneca became aware of these slanders, he tried to counteract their effect. What makes the story terrifying is that apparently there was absolutely nothing Seneca could do to stem the tide of events. He offered to withdraw from public life, and even to return the gifts and favors the emperor had given him. Nero was apparently most cordial to him, urged him to stay as his adviser, and refused to allow him to return the gifts. Tacitus concludes the story as follows:

To these words the emperor added embraces and kisses; for he was formed by nature and trained by habit to veil his hatred under delusive flattery. Seneca thanked him, the usual end of an interview with a despot. But he entirely altered the practices of his former greatness; he kept the crowds of his visitors at a distance, avoided trains of followers, seldom appeared in Rome, as though weak health or philosophical studies detained him at home. (p. 155a)

This is the end of the story, and a naïve reader might suppose that Seneca had either only imagined his troubles, or else had successfully coped with them by withdrawing from the emperor's presence. Such an illusion is shattered at once, for Tacitus with great directness begins the next paragraph thus:

"When Seneca had fallen . . ." Nor is this merely an instance of Tacitus' propensity for seeing the worst of everything. On page 168c he reports that Nero unsuccessfully tried to poison Seneca, and a few pages later we read that Nero used the occasion of Piso's conspiracy to accomplish his purpose.

Then followed the destruction of Annaeus Seneca, a special joy to the emperor, not because he had convicted him of the conspiracy, but anxious to accomplish with the sword what poison had failed to do. (p. 172c)

The phrase "a special joy to the emperor" reveals more about the character of Nero and Tacitus' opinion of him than a long harangue on the subject could do.

IV

Should Seneca share any of the blame for Nero's excesses?

The question may seem foolish at first, since Seneca himself suffered at Nero's hand and since, also, Seneca is famous as a Stoic. If there is anything that the Stoic philosophy is opposed to, it is excesses of passion such as Nero was given to; it teaches that reason should rule the passions and that the greatest good achievable by man is tranquillity of spirit.

Yet the question may be raised whether the Stoic philosophy provides sound guidance for an emperor. Seneca himself mentions this point in an essay entitled *On Mercy*, which is addressed to Nero himself. "I am aware," he writes, "that among the ill-informed the Stoic school is unpopular on the ground that it is excessively harsh and not at all likely to give good counsel to princes and kings; the criticism is made that it does not permit a wise man to be pitiful, does not permit him to pardon." Seneca goes on to acquit the Stoics of this charge by pointing out that the wise man will not pardon an offender in a capricious way by simply remitting deserved punishment. He will, however, fit the punishment to the crime and so will be merciful in the sense of being neither too harsh nor too lenient. He will take into account the circumstances of the crime, the age of the criminal, etc.

Though the elaboration of the doctrine does undoubtedly make good sense of it, it may be that Nero misunderstood it. He may only have retained the thought that pity as such is not a virtue, and that the wise man is not swayed in his judgment by such passions as pity. Consequently, he may have thought that it was a sign of wisdom on his part to be unyielding and cruel in his judgments. This is a point that cannot, of course, be proved or disproved.

In any case, the Seneca-Nero relationship is another instance of a philosopher-teacher and a ruler-pupil in which the pupil's actions do not live up to his teacher's precepts. We have already commented in the guide to the Second Reading on the relationship between Plato and Dionysius of Sicily, and between Aristotle and Alexander the Great.

Tacitus does not speak of Seneca's teachings as being too harsh for Nero or being misunderstood by the young emperor. On the contrary, he tells us that Burrus and Seneca indulged Nero when he first became emperor.

Burrus, with his soldier's discipline and severe manners, Seneca, with lessons of eloquence and a dignified courtesy, strove alike to confine the frailty of the prince's youth, should he loathe virtue, within allowable indulgences. (p. 126a)

If *this* account of the matter is correct, then perhaps Seneca would have served Nero and the empire better had he been more severe in his teaching. The doctrine which Tacitus here ascribes to Seneca, namely, that of allowing a little vice in order to prevent a craving for, and indulgence in, greater vices is certainly of dubious practical value, and most surely is not a Stoic doctrine at all.

Historical tradition (following Tacitus) generally paints Nero in the blackest colors. Are there any extenuating circumstances? Are there any good things that he did?

There certainly are some extenuating circumstances. For instance, Nero was not even seventeen years of age when he became emperor. His mother Agrippina was obviously very domineering and tried to exert her influence over him as much as possible. The environment in which he was brought up was rife with intrigue and treachery; in fact, Nero owed the throne to the machinations of his mother, who managed to get him proclaimed emperor in preference to Britannicus (his brother by adoption).

Furthermore, it can be seen that not everything that Nero did was unequivocally bad. Indeed, his reign started out in a rather promising fashion. Tacitus tells us:

> On the day of the funeral [Nero] pronounced Claudius's panegyric, and while he dwelt on the antiquity of his family and on the consulships and triumphs of his ancestors, there was enthusiasm both in himself and his audience. (p. 126a-b)

But later in the same paragraph Tacitus notes that Seneca composed the speech for Nero, and talks very disparagingly about Nero's other accomplishments. He begins the next paragraph by saying "When he had done with his mimicries of sorrow he entered the Senate . . ." Again, we can detect Tacitus' unwillingness to believe anything good about the emperors. As we saw earlier in the case of Tiberius, so here with Nero, Tacitus distrusts his motives and calls the funeral oration "mimicry." Funeral orations are, after all, never altogether true to their subject and indeed an orator who did not find laudatory things to say about a deceased person would be generally condemned, today no less than in antiquity.

Chapters 4 and 5 of Book XIII record the initial actions of Nero; they were not despotic but rather granted to the Senate more power than that body had had in recent years.

But it is the fire that nearly destroyed Rome which is the main basis for Nero's infamy. The rumor at once arose and never has ceased that the fire was started at Nero's own orders. (See Book XV, Chapters 38-44.) Tacitus mentions this rumor. However, it should be noted here that Tacitus is our most authentic source for these events (since he was closest in time to them), and that he indicates that it was not known in his time whether the fire was accidental or not. History, however, has generally overlooked Tacitus' doubt and has taken rumor for certainty.

None of this is to say, of course, that Nero was a person of spotless moral character. On the contrary, if you read the chapters assigned, you will have no difficulty in discovering any number of unquestionably odious and treacherous acts. But even in Nero's case there are a few things to be said on the other side. Historical evidence must always be sifted and evaluated.

Was the period described by Tacitus a successful one for the Roman empire?

If we were to judge merely by what Tacitus reports about the internal affairs of the state and its various turmoils, we would think that the Roman empire was on the brink of disaster. However, we must remember that the empire was far larger than Rome, and that all the troubles of the capital city were not reflected on the frontiers. For the most part the empire was secure, although there were always border wars, especially with the Germans in the west, and with the Parthians in the east.

On the whole, the empire maintained its size and strength unchanged from the time of Augustus to Nero. The greatest extent of the empire was reached about fifty years later, during the reign of Trajan (when Tacitus wrote).

Is imperial rule over colonies and dependencies compatible with constitutional government at home?

Tacitus is obviously nostalgic for the virtuous days of the Roman republic. But was this more than an empty dream? Is it possible for an empire as large as the Roman to be governed by anything but an absolute ruler? And does it follow that whenever a republic increases its size, its form of government is endangered? In the *Histories* Tacitus touches on this subject:

That old passion for power which has been ever innate in man increased and broke out as the Empire grew in greatness. In a state of moderate dimensions equality was easily preserved; but when the world had been subdued, when all rival kings and cities had been destroyed, and men had leisure to covet wealth which they might enjoy in security, the early conflicts between patricians and the people were kindled into flame. (p. 224d)

Does this mean that imperial expansion will lead to civil war because all want to share in the new luxuries? And is despotic rule the only way to avoid civil war?

Are there not contrary examples? Great Britain during the eighteenth and nineteenth centuries had a constitutional government at home while it was expanding its empire. Does this invalidate Tacitus' point? Is it relevant to this question that the Roman empire included "the world," that is, all civilized lands, while the British empire even at its height still had rivals?

Certainly there seems to be a feeling in the United States that there is much truth in Tacitus' thought. This feeling may help to explain the traditional American fear of entangling alliances or any form of empire building.

The following questions are designed to help you test the thoroughness of your reading. Each question is to be answered by giving a page or pages of the reading assignment. Answers will be found on page 220 of this Reading Plan.

1 According to Tacitus, what was the charge against the Christians in addition to that of setting fire to the city of Rome?

2 What was the amount of sales tax on slaves that Nero remitted?

3 Why was Gaius Caesar, the son of Agrippina and Germanicus, called Caligula?

4 How did Nero deal with his mother Agrippina when she tried to ally herself with his wife Octavia?

5 How did Agrippina die?

6 Whom did Nero marry after he divorced Octavia?

7 Who was the leader of the great conspiracy against Nero?

8 How did Seneca die?

AQUINAS

Summa Theologica

Part I–II, QQ. 90–97

Vol. 20, pp. 205–239

W ho is entitled to make laws for a society? What gives the laws their authority over us?

Everyone has asked himself these questions, for they are raised by the everyday contacts that each man has with the government under which he lives. But they are also questions which lie at the very heart of the philosophy of law and government; and the philosophical answers to them are connected with fundamental differences in political theory.

The answers which Aquinas gives to these questions rest on principles of right and justice and are opposed to answers which stem from the proposition that might makes right. All power and authority, in his view, ultimately come from God, but they do not pass directly from God to rulers to create kings by divine right. They are vested by God in the people as a whole. The power and authority which the people have from God to make the laws under which they live, they can either exercise directly or delegate to representatives of their own choosing. In either case, they are self-governing. They cannot rightly be subjected to laws laid down for them by one who wields political power without their consent and without duly constituted authority.

Here in Aquinas is one of the first clear statements of the doctrine of popular sovereignty. The voice of the people is the voice of God, but only when the people make just laws for the common good. Otherwise, popular sovereignty degenerates into the might of the majority, which is just another form of tyranny. But when, in addition to being made by duly constituted authority, the positive laws of the state are also based on the natural moral law and represent just regulations of human conduct, they speak with the authority of right, not just the force of might. While they exercise the sanction of coercive force over the bad man who obeys them only from fear of punishment, they bind the good man in conscience. In obeying them from the promptings of virtue he obeys them freely and not under coercion.

Sixth · Reading

I

This assignment consists of the opening questions of the *Treatise on Law*. This whole treatise is itself part of a much larger work known as the *Summa Theologica*. About two-thirds of the entire *Summa* are contained in Volumes 19 and 20 of our set. As the title indicates, it is a work in theology; it is intended to sum up, in condensed and relatively easy fashion, the theological doctrines of the Christian religion. In his Prologue to the entire work, Aquinas writes:

Because the teacher of catholic truth ought to teach not only those who have advanced along the road but also to instruct beginners . . . we purpose in this book to treat of whatever belongs to the Christian religion in a way that is suited to the instruction of beginners. (Vol. 19, p. 1a).

Since the *Treatise on Law* occurs near the middle of the *Summa Theologica,* it may be well to consider briefly the structure of the entire work and see where the *Treatise on Law* fits in.

The *Summa Theologica* is divided into three very large parts. Part I treats "of God," Part II treats "of the rational creature's movement towards God," and Part III treats "of Christ, Who as man, is our way to God" (Volume 19, p. 10c). Part II, in other words, deals with man in his theological and religious aspect. Or, to put it even more plainly, the second part of the *Summa* deals with happiness and man's efforts to achieve it; in his efforts to achieve happiness, man is moving toward God.

The second part of the *Summa* is again divided into two very large parts, known as the First Part of the Second Part, and the Second Part of the Second Part (usually designated as Part I-II and Part II-II). Part I-II deals with the means to happiness in general, and Part II-II deals with the means to happiness in particular.

Part I-II contains 114 questions. In the structure of the *Summa*, the question is the basic unit; and a treatise consists in a series of related questions. Thus, in Part I-II, questions 1-5 treat of the ultimate end of man. This is known as the *Treatise on the Last End*. Questions 6-48 treat of human acts. This is known as the *Treatise on Human Acts*. Next, Aquinas deals with the principles of human acts. This is known as the *Treatise on Habits*, which deals with all the virtues. After that Aquinas turns to the extrinsic principles of human acts. These principles are two in number: law (both human and divine) and God's grace. Accordingly, questions 90-108 treat of law and constitute the *Treatise on Law*. Questions 109-114 treat of grace and constitute the *Treatise on Grace*.

The *Treatise on Law* is divided into two parts. Questions 90-92 treat of law in general, while questions 93-108 treat of particular kinds of law. There we find that question 93 deals with the eternal law, question 94 with the natural law, questions 95-97 with the human law. Omitted from our reading are questions 98-105 dealing with the Old Law (*i.e.*, the law of the Old Testament), and questions 106-108 dealing with the New Law (the law of the New Testament).

II

Even though the *Summa Theologica* was written for the instruction of beginners, most people do not find it easy to read. There are several reasons for this. One certainly is that the "beginners" whom Aquinas had in mind were beginners in theology, but they were also students at the University of Paris, and had a good training in the liberal arts. Nevertheless, the questions and articles in the *Summa* are shorter and based on more easily grasped principles than the questions and articles in such a treatise as the *De Veritate*. In the latter, the reasoning is much more subtle, and an article may often contain fifteen or more objections.

This brings us to a second point of difficulty in reading the *Summa*. It consists in the structure of the articles. This difficulty can be easily overcome, however, if the reader will notice a few very simple things.

Each question in the *Summa* is divided into several articles. Actually, the title of the question is not in question form, but consists of a phrase like "Of the Natural Law" (which is the title of question 94). The several articles within a question are actually phrased as questions. Each is introduced by the word "whether." Thus, article 1 of question 94 is entitled "Whether the Natural Law Is a Habit?" and article 2 is "Whether the Natural Law Contains Several Precepts, or One Only?"

After the title, the article begins with "It would seem that the natural law is a habit" or "It would seem that the natural law contains not several precepts, but one only." These initial "it seems" statements usually indicate the opposite of Aquinas' conclusions. We can tell at once from them that it is Aquinas' opinion that natural law is *not* a habit, and that it contains *several* precepts. This is confirmed for us in the section beginning with "I answer that." Here we find Aquinas' own answer to the question, and it is the most important part of the whole article.

Preceding the answer, however, there are several objections, usually three or four. These objections are objections to the answer given by Aquinas; *i.e.*, they state and argue for positions that are opposed to Aquinas' own view. It is important to remember this. The objections give reasons why Aquinas' view seems to be false.

Following all the objections, there is a section that is introduced by the phrase "On the contrary." This usually contains quotations from one or more authorities, such as Scripture or St. Augustine. It always states a view contrary to that of the objections, and is, therefore, in accord with Aquinas' own view. But whereas the section beginning with the words "I answer that" sets forth rational arguments for the right answer, the section beginning with the words "On the contrary" merely offers an authoritative confirmation of it.

Finally, after the "I answer that" there follow Aquinas' argued replies to the objections, one for each objection.

In order not to become confused by the form of the article,

it seems best for the reader to proceed in the following fashion. *First*, notice the title of the article; this indicates the general subject to be discussed. *Second,* notice what, at the beginning, Aquinas says "seems" to be the case. The contrary of this will usually be Aquinas' own position. *Third*, proceed at once to read the portion commencing "I answer that." This will give Aquinas' own thought and his reasons for it. *Fourth*, return to the objections and read them together with their replies. Usually the replies will be based on the reasoning given in the answer.

III

St. Thomas Aquinas is a very systematic writer, hence it is hardly surprising that the first question in the *Treatise on Law* is entitled "Of the Essence of Law." In other words, this question deals with what law is. Notice that there is no reference to different kinds of law; the problem is what law—any law— is. Notice also that the entire discussion, although part of a theological treatise, is philosophical in character, not theological. There is no reference, in the answers of the four articles, to any biblical or patriarchal authority. The only author referred to is Aristotle, and the argument is based strictly on principles of reason, not of faith.

The first article establishes that a law is something pertaining to reason (*aliquid rationis*); in other words, a law is not something totally arbitrary or conventional, even though, as we shall see, there are elements of arbitrariness and conventionality in law.

The second article indicates the purpose for which law is instituted; namely, for the sake of the common good. Hence, a decree which may appear, in some respects, to be a law but which is not directed at the common good is not really a law. Thus Aquinas considers, a little later (in question 92, article 1, objection 4) the case of tyrannical laws:

Some laws are tyrannical . . . But a tyrant does not intend the good of his subjects, but considers only his own profit. (p. 213d)

He resolves this difficulty by saying:

A tyrannical law, since it is not in accordance with reason, is not a law, absolutely speaking, but rather a perversion of law . . . (p. 214c)

Next, Aquinas considers who has the authority to make a law:

A law, properly speaking, regards first and foremost the order to the common good. Now to order anything to the common good belongs either to the whole people, or to someone who is the vicegerent of the whole people. And therefore the making of a law belongs either to the whole people or to a public personage who has care of the whole people . . . (Q. 90, A. 3, Ans., p. 207b)

Finally, in article 4, Aquinas points out that a law must not only be properly made, but it must also be promulgated; that is, it must be made known to the men to whom it applies.

Aquinas concludes as follows:

Thus from the four preceding articles, the definition of law may be gathered; and it is nothing other than an ordinance of reason for the common good, made by him who has care of the community, and promulgated. (Q. 90, A. 4, Ans., p. 208a)

I V

From the essence of law in question 90, Aquinas turns to the kinds of law in question 91. In the six articles of this question, Aquinas distinguishes the following kinds of law.

Eternal law (article 1). This is the idea of the government of things in God. Notice that here, unlike question 90, theological and religious concepts are employed.

Natural law (article 2). All things are governed by natural law, since all things are governed by eternal law. The natural law is the imprint of the eternal law on things "in so far as, namely, from its being imprinted on them, they derive their respective inclinations to their proper acts and ends" (p. 209b).

Human law (article 3), often called "positive law." Human law is needed because "from the precepts of the natural law, as from general and indemonstrable principles . . . the human reason needs to proceed to the more particular determination of certain matters. These particular determinations, devised by human reason, are called human laws, provided the other essential conditions of law be observed" (p. 210a).

Divine law, often called "divine positive law" to distinguish it from the eternal law. These are the direct (or positive) pronouncements of God, such as the Ten Commandments. Divine law, therefore, is itself of two kinds, namely the *Old Law* (article 4) and the *New Law* (article 5).

Finally, in article 6, Aquinas declares that in a certain way there is even a law of sin. (Since this is a rather special consideration, we shall not pay any further attention to it.)

Let us try to understand these four different kinds of law by means of an example. Consider the prohibition against murder. Murder is forbidden by the natural law, by the human law, and by the divine law. Why is one and the same kind of act forbidden by different laws? Does each law deal with murder in exactly the same way?

Let us begin with the natural law. How does it prohibit murder? One thing is clear at once. The natural law is not written. Consequently, the natural law must be promulgated in a rather special way. This raises the question whether the natural law is law at all. For if it is not written down, how can the natural law be promulgated, as the definition of law says it should be? In question 90, article 4, objection 1, this objection is raised and Aquinas answers it as follows:

The natural law is promulgated by the very fact that God instilled it into man's mind so as to be known by him naturally. (p. 208a)

Is it then instilled by God into man's mind that he should not murder? We must avoid thinking that the precepts of the natural law are "written" in the heart or mind of man in some literal fashion, so that man merely has to "look" in his heart or mind and there find noted down everything he is to do or to avoid.

In question 94, article 2, Aquinas tells us, instead, that

the order of the precepts of the natural law is according to the order of natural inclinations. (p. 222c)

Since man is a rational creature

there is in man an inclination to good, according to the nature of his reason, which nature is proper to him; thus man has a natural inclination to know the truth about God, and to live in society. And in this respect, whatever pertains to this inclination belongs to the natural law; for instance, to shun ignorance, to avoid offending those among whom one has to live, and other such things regarding the above inclination. (p. 222d)

The precepts of the natural law, therefore, are in man as inclinations in accord with his nature. The prohibition against murder, therefore, is part of man's natural inclination to live in society (for the sake of happiness), which implies everything that is needed in order to live in society, particularly the injunction to avoid harming others.

This way of viewing the natural law helps us to understand why there is, in addition, a divine positive law which prohibits murder. As part of the natural law, the prohibition against murder is merely implicit. Everyone may not readily recognize it as implied by man's desire and need to live in society. The divine positive law, therefore, removes any doubt on this point by unequivocally declaring "Thou shalt not kill." This, however, is only one reason why there is a divine law; in question 91, article 4 ("Whether There Was Any Need for a Divine Law") Aquinas gives us four reasons for having divine law in addition to natural law.

Granted, then, that the natural law forbids killing by implication, and that the divine positive law makes this explicit, what further need is there for the human law and its injunction against killing? This question, too, is considered in question 91, article 3. Aquinas concludes that there is need for human law, because the natural law is general in its precepts but needs to be applied to particular cases.

From the precepts of the natural law, as from general and indemonstrable principles . . . the human reason needs to proceed to the more particular determination of certain matters. These particular determinations, devised by human reason, are called human laws, provided the other essential conditions of law be observed . . . (p. 210a-b)

We can easily see the need for particular determinations in the case of the law against murder. Murder is forbidden by natural and divine law; but what is murder? Clearly, not any killing is murder, for not all killing is unlawful. In self-defense, a man may kill; in war, killing is not only permitted but

actually commanded (even the children of Israel were sometimes commanded by God to kill their enemies). And again,
though most killing is forbidden, not all of it is considered as
punishable to the same degree. The human law, therefore,
distinguishes between two and sometimes three degrees of
murder, the distinctions being based largely on the degree of
deliberate intent.

Human law, therefore, is an application of natural law by
way of determining concretely what the natural law leaves
undetermined. It is less general than the natural law and more
adapted to particular circumstances. It is clear that the greater
particularity of the human law is also the reason why the
number of precepts in the human law is much greater than in
the natural law.

Here again it must be remembered that when we call human
law an application of natural law, we are only speaking of just
laws (that is, laws in which "the other essential conditions of
law [are] observed"). Unjust laws, like tyrannical laws, are, as
we saw above, laws in name only.

V

Is every human law derived from the natural law?

We have said above that human law must be instituted,
because the natural law is too general. That would seem to
imply that every human law is derived from some precept of
the natural law. Yet there are certain obvious difficulties with
this position.

For instance, it is a positive law in the United States that
cars must drive on the right side of the road. But how can such
a traffic ordinance be said to be derived from the natural law,
since obviously it could just as well have been laid down that
everyone should drive on the left side of the road, and in many
countries, including Great Britain, this is indeed the case.

Again, if every human law is derived from natural law, why
do we distinguish between the two of them? Why is not all
law simply natural law, though some laws are perhaps general
natural laws, and others particular natural laws?

Then too, if all human law is derived from natural law, and if all natural law is everywhere the same, human law should be the same everywhere also. But that is obviously not the case, since the human laws of different countries differ in many respects and yet all may be just.

Finally, the question may be put in this way: If the natural law says what the tendency of human nature is, and if human nature has the character of rational animality (as Aquinas would maintain), then all natural law for man must be based on the reasonableness of human nature. But there is nothing more reasonable about driving on the right than on the left side of the road.

In spite of all these difficulties, Aquinas maintains that every human law is derived from natural law. He gets around the difficulties we have raised by pointing out that the derivation may be of two kinds. Some human laws are derived from the natural law in the way in which a conclusion is derived from premises; other human laws, however, are derived as determinations of generalities. He writes:

Some things are therefore derived from the common principles of the natural law by way of conclusions; for instance, that one must not kill may be derived as a conclusion from the principle that one should do harm to no man. But some are derived from these principles by way of determination; for instance, the law of nature has it that the evil-doer should be punished, but that he be punished in this or that way is a determination of the law of nature. (p. 228a-b)

Here, then, we see how a certain arbitrariness enters into human law, even though it is derived from the natural law. What is strictly a precept of natural law (such as "Do harm to no man") is certainly a proposition of reason; but when a human law is instituted as a determination of natural law (as, for example, whether cars should drive on the right or the left side of the road), that determination proceeds from the will of the lawgiver and so is not *entirely* a proposition of reason but has something of the character of an arbitrary fiat. Such a law represents the *arbitrium* (Latin for "judgment" or "will") of the lawgiver. It is obviously in accordance with the natural law that all cars should drive *on the same side* of the road (as a simple conclusion from the premise that man should harm no one, including himself); but there is no way to derive the conclusion as to which side it should be. Yet, since it must be decided one way or the other, the lawgiver must arbitrarily make the determination in one way. Once that determination has been made, it has the force of a law that is derived from the natural law by way of conclusion.

All the difficulties which we have raised, therefore, can easily be solved. They were all based on the assumption that human laws are derived from natural law as conclusions are derived from premises.

You may also be interested in observing that in the foregoing paragraphs we have very nearly produced article 2 of question 95 (see pp. 227c-228c). If you look back on what you have just read, you will see that, although we did not label the parts of our argument, they do divide into four objections, after which we propose our "I answer that . . ." The only thing we omitted was the "On the contrary . . ." and the replies to the objections. Perhaps the arrangement of an article in the *Summa* will not seem quite so strange and confusing to you after this.

Are human laws sufficiently particular to be applicable to all situations and circumstances?

We have noted that the human law is more specific in its application than the natural law, and that many things which are indifferent so far as the natural law is concerned are nevertheless decided in a particular fashion by the human law because it is necessary that some decision be made. But now the question is whether human law is particular enough to deal with any and all particular circumstances.

It is easy to see that a law is supposed to be applicable to many situations or cases; otherwise, there would have to be a separate law for every case. Consequently, a law cannot be so particular as to take into account every circumstance. Rather than being applicable to only one case, a law is applicable to a kind of case. To give an extreme example, no law can be imagined that would say "Mr. X shall not murder Mr. Y on Wednesday, April 19, 1961." That would require an infinite number of other laws, prohibiting murder on other dates and by other men. Such circumstances as time, place and the particular men involved are usually, therefore, irrelevant details. Aquinas explains this point as follows:

Human laws should be proportionate to the common good. Now the common good comprises many things. Therefore law should take account of many things, as to persons, as to matters, and as to times. Because the community of the state is composed of many persons, and its good is procured by many actions; nor is it established to endure for only a short time, but to last for all time by the citizens succeeding one another. (p. 231a)

Who is authorized to make human laws?

In the definition of law (question 90, article 4) we read that law is "made by him who has care of the community." Who, then, has care of the community? Does the fact that Aquinas speaks of "him" indicate that he necessarily has a single person in mind, like a king? Is his argument concerning law inapplicable to forms of government other than monarchy?

Let us answer the second question first. Though Aquinas speaks of a lawgiver in the singular person, there is nothing in his argument that makes it inapplicable to a lawgiving assembly. In fact, he says very little about the lawgiver, beyond indicating that there must be such a person or such an authority, and that it is not just anybody who is authorized to make laws, but only he "who has care of the community."

But the care of the community, Aquinas tells us,

belongs either to the whole people, or to someone who is the vicegerent of the whole people. And therefore the making of a law belongs either to the whole people or to a public personage who has care of the whole people . . . (p. 207b)

Thus Aquinas recognizes the possibility that the lawgiver might be the whole community. In fact, in question 97, article 3, he envisages a situation in which the lawgiving function is taken over by the whole community. He did not, of course, envisage a popular government. He did not envisage that the community as a whole would make laws as a regular constitutional process. But he does see that it might happen occasionally and that it would then be legitimate. Repeated customary actions on the part of the whole community, his argument goes, gradually acquire the force of law, even if they have never been written or officially instituted as laws by a king or a similar personage:

> By actions also, especially if they be repeated, so as to make a custom, law can be changed and expressed; and also something can be established which obtains force of law, in so far as by repeated external actions the inward movement of the will, and concepts of reason are most effectually declared. For when a thing is done again and again, it seems to proceed from a deliberate judgment of reason. Accordingly, custom has the force of a law, abolishes law, and is the interpreter of law. (p. 237d)

Can the natural law be changed?

Here it would seem as if the answer must be immediately and unequivocally No. If the nature of man cannot change, then neither can the natural law for man, which is nothing but a statement of the tendencies and inclinations of his nature. This is certainly the first and correct answer. It is especially true that nothing can be subtracted from the natural law. If something is commanded or prohibited by the natural law, then it is so commanded or prohibited forever.

This, of course, is not to say that sometimes men may not misapprehend what the natural law commands. In many ambiguous cases the ambiguity is resolved through the explicit commands of the divine positive law. But there may still be some cases where human reason misunderstands what its own proper inclinations are. When such misunderstandings are cleared up, that is not a change in the natural law, but rather a change in our understanding of it.

There may, however, be additions to the natural law. "Many things for the benefit of human life have been added over and above the natural law, both by the Divine law and by human laws" (p. 225b). This occurs in situations where the natural law does not explicitly state the contrary. "In this sense," Aquinas says, " 'the possession of all things in common, and uniform freedom' are said to be of the natural law, because, that is, the distinction of possessions [*i.e.*, private property] and slavery were not brought in by nature, but devised by human reason for the benefit of human life" (p. 225d).

The following questions are designed to help you test the thoroughness of your reading. Each question is to be answered by giving a page or pages of the reading assignment. Answers will be found on page 220 of this Reading Plan.

1 What are the various acts of law?

2 How can there be a variation in natural law?

3 What is the law of nations (*ius gentium*)?

4 Does human law, in addition to being enforced by the threat of punishment, also bind a man in conscience?

5 How is the eternal law promulgated to natural, nonrational things?

6 What is the distinction between laws that make men good absolutely and laws that make men good relatively?

7 Why is it better that things be regulated by laws than by judges judging without laws?

8 Is the sovereign exempt from the law?

9 Is a good man coerced by the law?

MACHIAVELLI

The Prince

Vol. 23, pp. 1–37

T his little book is the first and greatest in a long line of works which deal with how men gain and hold political power. It was written in the sixteenth century by an out-of-office administrator and diplomat of the city-state of Florence. Behind its astute analysis lie years of firsthand experience of contemporary political life and a careful study of ancient political history.

This potent pamphlet is in the form of a how-to-do-it book for a ruler or would-be ruler. It tells how to become a successful, not a good or wise, ruler. The successful politician should be concerned with having a good reputation, not with being virtuous. If he has to choose between being feared or loved, he will find it better to be feared. He must be like a lion and a fox, employing force and deceit. If successful, he will win popular approval, and his villainies will be forgotten. Nothing succeeds like success.

This is an astonishing break with classical political

thought, which links politics and ethics. Aristotle was an objective student of politics, but he saw political rule as having ethical ends. The modern departure, fathered by Machiavelli, regards ethical judgments as irrelevant in the scientific approach to politics, which should inquire into the "how" of things as they are. We cannot help being fascinated by this masterful analysis of the facts of political life, whatever our moral qualms or reservations. We who have lived in an era of astute "princes," from Lenin to Franco, naturally read Machiavelli as if he were a commentator on the contemporary scene. An age which has known Hitler, Mussolini, and Stalin, and experienced bluff, terror, propaganda, and "cold war" has therefore experienced all the political realities with which Machiavelli deals; but it can still learn to understand them better and, perhaps, to question how far sheer power politics can ever succeed.

Seventh Reading

I

Niccolo Machiavelli was born in Florence in 1469 and died there in 1527. Thus he was located, both with respect to time and place, at the heart of the Renaissance. It is not altogether easy to say just what the Renaissance was, nor when it began and when it ended. But we may safely say that it was a period of transition from the middle ages to modern times, that it included a revival of learning, and that it was accompanied by political and religious turmoil. In Italy, where the Renaissance achieved its greatest flowering, it began sometime after 1350 and was definitely over by 1550.

It may help us to visualize this period if we recall some of the great names of the Italian Renaissance. There were such artists as Leonardo da Vinci, Michelangelo, and Raphael; such political leaders as Lorenzo de' Medici and Cesare Borgia; such churchmen as Pope Alexander VI and the Florentine friar Savonarola; adventurers and explorers like Christopher Columbus and Amerigo Vespucci; philosophers like Pico della Mirandola, Pomponazzi, and Giordano Bruno.

At the center of the Renaissance in Italy stood Florence. Jacob Burckhardt describes the city thus:

The most elevated political thought and the most varied forms of human development are found united in the history of Florence, which in this sense deserves the name of the first modern State in the world. Here the whole people are busied with what in the despotic cities is the affair of a single family. That wondrous Florentine spirit, at once keenly critical and artistically creative, was incessantly transforming the social and political condition of the State, and as incessantly describing and judging the change. Florence thus became the home of political doctrines and theories, of experiments and sudden changes . . . (*The Civilization of the Renaissance in Italy,* New York, 1945, p. 48)

In the midst of this hotbed of political thought and action, Machiavelli lived and wrote. For the details of his life we refer the reader to the Biographical Note (pp. ix-x), but here is Burckhardt's evaluation of him:

But of all who thought it possible to construct a State, the greatest beyond all comparison was Machiavelli. He treats existing forces as living and active, takes a large and an accurate view of alternative possibilities, and seeks to mislead neither himself nor others. No man could be freer from vanity or ostentation; indeed, he does not write for the public, but either for princes and administrators or for personal friends. The danger for him does not lie in an affectation of genius or in a false order of ideas, but rather in a powerful imagination which he evidently controls with difficulty. The objectivity of his political judgement is sometimes appalling in its sincerity; but it is the sign of a time of no ordinary need and peril, when it was a hard matter to believe in right, or to credit others with just dealing. (*Ibid.*, pp. 54-55)

II

In spite of such high praise, the adjective "Machiavellian" as it is commonly used has derogatory connotations. Generally a man is considered to be "Machiavellian" if he is crafty, cunning, and unscrupulous. A man of such character is supposed to be Machiavelli's ideal.

Let us examine Machiavelli's aims and the means he proposes to reach that end. At the very outset it is clear that Machiavelli is not drawing a picture of an ideal man. His book is not addressed to all of mankind; it is rather meant only for a prince or king. In fact, *The Prince* is dedicated to a prince of the Medici family (see the dedication on p. 1).

Again, *The Prince* is not a theoretical exposition of its subject, as, for example, the *Treatise on Law* is. Rather, it is a practical political treatise; that is to say, it is directed toward action. How does Machiavelli's work compare with other practical political writing that we have read, such as Aristotle's *Politics?* The guiding principle of Machiavelli's writing is the following statement, taken not from *The Prince*, but from another book:

Whoever desires to found a state and give it laws, must start with assuming that all men are bad and ever ready to display their vicious nature, whenever they may find occasion for it. (*Discourses*, Book I, Ch. 3)

This statement is not, of course, very flattering to man. Nevertheless, it may well be correct that practical political action takes its beginning from it. Certainly there is much evidence that states deal with one another in a fashion that is based precisely on some such assumption. Power politics, *Realpolitik*, "brink-of-war-policies" are all based on the hypothesis that sovereign states (and presumably the people composing them) are concerned solely with survival and domination and respect nothing but force or the threat of force.

Machiavelli can find support in other writers for his position. He himself attributes the above statement to "all those who have written upon civil institutions" and adds that "history is full of examples to support them."

Thus, Aristotle's *Politics* contains support for Machiavelli. "Man," says Aristotle in Chapter 2,

when perfected, is the best of animals, but, when separated from law and justice, he is the worst of all; since armed injustice is the more dangerous, and he is equipped at birth with arms, meant to be used by intelligence and virtue, which he may use for the worst ends. Wherefore, if he have not virtue, he is the most unholy and the most savage of animals, and the most full of lust and gluttony. (Vol. 9, p. 446d)

But if this is a correct description of man, then Machiavelli might be justified in looking for any means that will preserve law and order, if not justice, in the state.

The same low opinion of man is reflected in the *Republic*, although the position is not espoused by Socrates, but by Glaucon, who tells the story of the ring of Gyges. He concludes the fable thus:

For all men believe in their hearts that injustice is far more profitable to the individual than justice, and he who argues as I have been supposing, will say that they are right. If you could imagine any one obtaining this power of becoming invisible, and never doing any wrong or touching what was another's, he would be thought by the lookers-on to be a most wretched idiot ... (Vol. 7, p. 312a-b)

Machiavelli, therefore, is simply dealing with men as they are, not as they should be. He is under no illusion that the methods which he advocates are noble. For in discussing Agathocles, a tyrant of Sicily, who successfully obtained his position through bloodshed and violence, he adds:

> Yet it cannot be called talent to slay fellow-citizens, to deceive friends, to be without faith, without mercy, without religion; such methods may gain empire, but not glory. (p. 13b)

In spite of this, he thinks that the skill and cleverness of Agathocles are to be highly esteemed:

> Nevertheless, his barbarous cruelty and inhumanity with infinite wickednesses do not permit him to be celebrated among the most excellent men. (p. 13c)

Both Plato and Aristotle want to check man's bestiality. Plato proposed to do it through education; Aristotle through the state and law. Both of these, of course, are long-range projects. Machiavelli, concerned with man's present brutality, suggests to the prince that he combat his subjects' bestiality by becoming a stronger and more clever beast himself. In a famous passage he says:

> . . . there are two ways of contesting, the one by the law, the other by force; the first method is proper to men, the second to beasts; but because the first is frequently not sufficient, it is necessary to have recourse to the second . . . A prince, therefore, being compelled knowingly to adopt the beast, ought to choose the fox and the lion; because the lion cannot defend himself against snares and the fox cannot defend himself against wolves. Therefore, it is necessary to be a fox to discover the snares and a lion to terrify the wolves. (p. 25a-b)

III

Is Machiavelli's advice sound? Will a prince be likely to stay in power by following it?

For most of us the soundness (or lack of soundness) of Machiavelli's advice will, of course, remain a matter of conjecture. We are not likely to be princes and so will not be able to put his advice into practice. However, if we wish to test Machiavelli's suggestions, we may imagine what we would say to a prince if *we* were placed in an advisory capacity.

In Chapter X, Machiavelli advises the prince to fortify his cities. This, in Machiavelli's opinion, will deter potential invaders and he tells us why:

Men are always adverse to enterprises where difficulties can be seen, and it will be seen not to be an easy thing to attack one who has his town well fortified, and is not hated by his people. (p. 16b)

Machiavelli's advice is, of course, tailored to the conditions of the fifteenth century. Nevertheless, the policy which the United States is following in the twentieth century seems to be not too different. Like Machiavelli's prince, the United States is fortifying itself; *i.e.*, building up its defenses so that a potential aggressor will be deterred. At the same time, the United States is trying to keep the good will of allies all over the world.

Consider another, more extreme, piece of advice. This is taken from the beginning of Chapter XIV:

A prince ought to have no other aim or thought, nor select anything else for his study, than war and its rules and discipline; for this is the sole art that belongs to him who rules, and it is of such force that it not only upholds those who are born princes, but it often enables men to rise from a private station to that rank. (p. 21b)

Is this cynicism on Machiavelli's part? Or is this sound practical advice? Should the sole concern of princes, rulers, or governments be war? Are there any arts of peace that should also be learned by rulers? Is it as important to "wage peace" as it is to wage war?

Is The Prince *an immoral book?*

If the book is immoral it must be because it advocates immoral actions. Does it do that? While its premise, that political thinking must be guided by the fact that men are bad, is not shared by such writers as Aristotle and Plato, there are many passages in their works that take a realistic view of politics. Aristotle, for example, in Book V of the *Politics*, gives advice to tyrants on how they should act in order to preserve their tyrannies. All of Book V is concerned with revolutions in various types of states and the ways of avoiding them. In Chapter 11, Aristotle turns to monarchies and tyrannies. He evidently considered it perfectly proper for a political treatise to consider how a tyrant should act to maintain himself in power. The advice which he gives is interesting, too. In general,

Aristotle advocates two sorts of action. The first sort is what he calls "the old traditional method in which most tyrants administer their government." This calls for the tyrant to "put to death men of spirit," to "employ spies," "to sow quarrels among the citizens," to "impoverish his subjects," "to distrust his friends," and other similar actions. The second sort of action that Aristotle advocates is different. Here he advises the tyrant to practice virtue or at least a quasi-virtue, so that the citizens will love and not hate him. The first sort of action advocated by Aristotle is certainly "Machiavellian," and even the second sort is not altogether contrary to the spirit of *The Prince*, since Machiavelli emphasizes that it is good for the prince to be loved, if that can be accomplished without jeopardizing his power which rests mainly on fear. (See Chapter XVII.)

Even in Plato we find much that sounds like Machiavelli's thought. For instance, compare the following two passages. The first is from *The Prince*, Chapter XVIII, entitled "Concerning the Way in Which Princes Should Keep Faith."

Therefore it is unnecessary for a prince to have all the good qualities I have enumerated, but it is very necessary to appear to have them. And I shall dare to say this also, that to have them and always to observe them is injurious, and that to appear to have them is useful. (p. 25c)

The next passage is from the *Republic*, Book II. Glaucon, after having told the story of the ring of Gyges, maintains that the eulogists of injustice will speak as follows:

They will tell you that the just man who is thought unjust will be scourged, racked, bound—will have his eyes burnt out; and, at last, after suffering every kind of evil, he will be impaled: Then he will understand that he ought to seem only, and not to be, just. (Vol. 7, p. 312d)

This, to be sure, is not Plato's or Socrates' position. But Plato himself is not above using questionable means to attain his political ends. He is willing to recommend the so-called "royal lie," which we discussed in the guide to the first assignment of this Reading Plan. Plato, it will be remembered, saw nothing wrong with telling a lie to the citizens of his ideal state, so that each one would be satisfied with his station and his duties. (See Vol. 7, pp. 340b-341b.)

Is there any difference, then, between *The Prince,* the *Republic,* and the *Politics,* or are all three alike immoral books concerned merely with political expediency? The question almost answers itself. Though all three books are alike in being political and practical and in dealing with the *means* needed to accomplish political ends, there is a great difference in the *ends* which they advocate. Plato's purpose was the discovery of justice and the establishment of a perfectly just state. That purpose certainly is highly moral and laudable, whatever we may think of some of the means involved. Aristotle's *Politics* is a direct continuation of his moral treatise, the *Ethics.* Far from considering the state and its laws as things that concern only the rulers, he considers the state necessary for human happiness and thinks that the constitution is man's salvation. All of his remarks, therefore, must be understood as being governed by the essential moral role which he feels the state plays in man's life.

But *The Prince* is altogether different in its purpose. We can discover no moral end that Machiavelli's remarks are to serve. There seems to be, in fact, no end that he has in mind except that of *success.* Machiavelli's maxim seems to be that everything is permissible as long as it succeeds. There is no concern with *why* men should live in states, *why* rulers should govern in one way or another, *why* certain means should be employed and others not. Consequently, though some of Machiavelli's advice may be useful to the best of rulers, some or all of it can also be used by the worst tyrants and dictators. *The Prince* would seem to be, then, at best an *amoral* book, and at worst, actually *immoral.*

Does the last chapter of The Prince *state a moral end that can justify it?*

It is sometimes maintained that the moral end for which we were just now looking is supplied in the last chapter of the book ("An Exhortation to Liberate Italy from the Barbarians"). Perhaps a case can be made for Machiavelli here. For the first time in the book, he here sets forth a worthy and patriotic goal which his treatise on political means can serve.

Some doubts remain, however, since this twenty-sixth chapter seems like an appendage to the book and since, also, it is addressed to the house of Medici. An interesting sentence occurs in the middle of the chapter. Machiavelli tells us that "that war is just which is necessary" (p. 36d). Is this the sentiment of justice or of expediency? How does it compare with the very opposite view—that war is necessary which is just?

The reader will have to judge Machiavelli's morality or immorality for himself.

Is Machiavelli's advice suitable not only for princes, but also for statesmen in republics?

Is it good advice for the elected heads of republics that "the chief foundation of all states . . . are good laws and good arms; and as there cannot be good laws where the state is not well armed, it follows that where they are well armed they have good laws" (p. 18a).

Is it correct to say that such a statesman "ought to have no other aim or thought . . . than war"? (p. 21b).

Could we substitute the word "statesman" in the following assertion and accept it: "It is necessary for a prince wishing to hold his own to know how to do wrong"? (p. 22b).

What is Machiavelli's view of the role of fortune in human life?

This is a question that must be answered by any historian or writer on political subjects who draws heavily (as Machiavelli does) on historical example and precedent. The study of history will often give rise to the suspicion that the actions of men (at least the large and important actions) are not really under their control but that men are buffeted about by fortune, though they may have the illusion that they direct their own lives.

If all, or at least all large-scale, human events are matters of fortune, then, of course, it is useless to write books such as *The Prince*. Machiavelli's fundamental assumption certainly is that the prince can do something about the events that take place.

Does there seem to be any plausibility in the way in which he apportions the roles of fortune and free will?

Nevertheless, not to extinguish our free will, I hold it to be true that Fortune is the arbiter of one-half of our actions, but that she still leaves us to direct the other half, or perhaps a little less. (p. 35a-b)

The following questions are designed to help you test the thoroughness of your reading. Each question is to be answered by giving a page or pages of the reading assignment. Answers will be found on page 220 of this Reading Plan.

1 Does Machiavelli consider mercenaries to be trustworthy soldiers?

2 In a war between neighboring states, should a prince or state take sides or be neutral?

3 How should a prince commit those cruelties that are necessary if he is usurping power?

4 What should a prince do to exercise his intellect?

5 How did Hannibal avoid mutiny in his army?

6 How must a conqueror deal with cities that had republican government?

7 Should a prince keep his word?

8 What does Machiavelli think of flattery?

9 Should a prince wish to be loved or feared?

HOBBES

Leviathan

Introduction and Chapters 13–21

Vol. 23, pp. 47, 84–117

T homas Hobbes is a strange phenomenon in the history of political philosophy. We expect an emphasis on individual rights and a fear of absolute power from the English-speaking writers. But the main concern of Hobbes was peace and order. For that boon he was willing to forgo many kinds of liberty. He felt that justice and elementary freedom could only exist under a practically omnipotent government.

When he thought of man in a state of nature, without civil society, Hobbes saw an appalling picture. There was a war of all against all, no one could feel safe, fear and anxiety were always present. This was not just a matter of actual conflict and rapine, but also of constant tension, as in the "cold war" between sovereign nations. Hobbes was presciently aware of that delicate international condition which prevails in the middle of the twentieth century.

Hobbes does not glorify absolute power. He sees it as a matter of necessity for individual self-preservation. This is a marriage of convenience, in which individuals give up the uncertain pleasures of single liberty for the security of communal life. It is a matter of enlightened self-interest.

Hobbes wrote this book to aid the Royalist side during the English Civil Wars. But astute Royalists saw that it took the divine aura away from kingship. Ironically, it was not authoritarian Royalists, but liberal thinkers, aiming at a social order based on enlightened self-interest, who became the philosophic heirs of Hobbes.

Eighth Reading

I

Thomas Hobbes was born in 1588, sixty-one years after the death of Machiavelli. He lived for ninety-one years, and died on December 4, 1679. His lifetime encompassed one of the most turbulent periods in English history. He was born during the reign of Queen Elizabeth I, and lived through the reigns of James I, Charles I, through the period of the Commonwealth and Oliver Cromwell, and on into the reign of Charles II.

Hobbes was of a timid disposition; he felt that his views of sovereignty and monarchy made it dangerous for him to be in England during the struggle between king and Parliament. That is why he spent eleven years in self-imposed exile, mostly in Paris. However, he returned to England in 1651, while Cromwell was still in power, and lived unharmed. After the Restoration, King Charles II protected Hobbes who had at one time been his teacher.

In spite of royal favor, however, Hobbes had difficulty in getting his work published. He was suspected of teaching atheism in his books; for instance, in the *Leviathan* (which had been published in 1651). Hobbes's last writings, therefore, had to be published in Amsterdam. For a more complete account of his life, see the Biographical Note (pp. 41-42) and the article HOBBES in *Encyclopædia Britannica*.

Modern political thought stems from Hobbes. Indeed, we may designate the year 1600 as the approximate point in time at which characteristic trends in all fields of modern thought begin to emerge. Modern philosophy very largely takes its beginning from Hobbes's contemporary Descartes. Modern science is also initiated at this time with the work of such men as Bacon, Boyle, Harvey, and Galileo.

II

What is it that is distinctly new and modern in Hobbes's political thought? His political theory is built around the notion of a *state of nature*. This conception is not found in earlier political writers, but hardly any of Hobbes's successors could do without it. The state of nature plays an important role in the writings of John Locke, Jean Jacques Rousseau, and Immanuel Kant.

By "state of nature" Hobbes means a time in which men lived without any government; a primitive condition in which there was no king, no law, and no civil society. Hobbes believes that men once actually lived in this condition; most of his successors consider the state of nature as a hypothetical notion needed to explain the origin of civil society. "It may peradventure be thought," Hobbes writes,

there was never such a time nor condition . . . as this; and I believe it was never generally so, over all the world: but there are many places where they live so now. For the savage people in many places of America, except the government of small families, the concord whereof dependeth on natural lust, have no government at all, and live at this day in that brutish manner, as I said before. (pp. 85d-86a)

Even if there were no such savage peoples, we should still have examples of the state of nature:

But though there had never been any time wherein particular men were in a condition of war one against another, yet in all times kings and persons of sovereign authority, because of their independency, are in continual jealousies, and in the state and posture of gladiators, having their weapons pointing, and their eyes fixed on one another; that is, their forts, garrisons, and guns upon the frontiers of their kingdoms, and continual spies upon their neighbours, which is a posture of war. (p. 86a)

These explanations by Hobbes of where the state of nature is to be found give us a hint of the character of this state of nature. In short, *the state of nature is a state of war.* "During the time men live without a common power to keep them all in awe, they are in that condition which is called *war*" (p. 85b). The reason for this is that man is competitive, yet diffident, and also desirous of glory. All three characteristics cause men to fight: the first, in order to gain someone else's possessions; the second, to protect his own; the third, to obtain fame and reputation. Therefore, as long as men are not kept from fighting by fear of some stronger power,

they are in that condition which is called *war*; and such a war as is of every man against every man. (p. 85b)

To be in a state of war, Hobbes continues, it is not necessary for men to be actually fighting all the time. It suffices that each man is ready to fight, whenever he thinks that it will be advantageous to him. Constant threat of combat, in other words, is itself a kind of war.

For war consisteth not in battle only, or the act of fighting, but in a tract of time, wherein the will to contend by battle is sufficiently known: and therefore the notion of *time* is to be considered in the nature of war, as it is in the nature of weather. For as the nature of foul weather lieth not in a shower or two of rain, but in an inclination thereto of many days together: so the nature of war consisteth not in actual fighting, but in the known disposition thereto during all the time there is no assurance to the contrary. All other time is *peace*. (p. 85b-c)

This description by Hobbes fits perfectly what we are accustomed to call the "cold war." The "cold war," he maintains, is as much war as a "hot war." We have already noted that Hobbes thinks that kings and sovereign states are in a state of nature (or state of war) with respect to each other. Since they are not always in actual combat, Hobbes clearly thought that the sovereign states in the seventeenth century were as much in a condition of "cold war" as the United States and Russia are in the twentieth.

It takes very little imagination to see that man's condition in such a state of war—of everyone against everyone—must be miserable. Few, however, have ever described this state as eloquently as Hobbes did:

Whatsoever therefore is consequent to a time of war, where every man is enemy to every man, the same is consequent to the time wherein men live without other security than what their own strength and their own invention shall furnish them withal. In such condition there is no place for industry, because the fruit thereof is uncertain: and consequently no culture of the earth; no navigation, nor use of the commodities that may be imported by sea; no commodious building; no instruments of moving and removing such things as require much force; no knowledge of the face of the earth; no account of time; no arts; no letters; no society; and which is worst of all, continual fear, and danger of violent death; and the life of man, solitary, poor, nasty, brutish, and short. (p. 85c)

If we think of this description as applying to individual men, we no doubt feel sorry for them and would advise them to quit this miserable condition. But we should also remember that this description must be applicable to the condition of sovereign nations, since they live in a state of war. Hobbes, therefore, by implication tells us that the life of such nations is one of continual fear, that they are in constant danger of coming to a violent end, and that each one lives solitarily in a fashion that is "poor, nasty, brutish, and short." If Hobbes's description is correct and if it is applicable to the life of nations, then whatever arguments he has for urging men to quit the state of nature apply with equal force to nations in their present state of war.

III

Should men, then, quit the state of nature or war? Hobbes's answer is an emphatic Yes. His affirmation is drawn from the *natural law*. Reason tells us, according to Hobbes, that everyone should try to live in peace; if that, however, is not possible, then everyone naturally must try to wage war as advantageously as possible.

Thus, he continues, the first law or command of nature is: *to seek peace and follow it.* But if peace is unobtainable, then we also have by nature this right: *to defend ourselves by any means we can.*

From the first law of nature which commands peace, there follows the second law of nature:

that a man be willing, when others are so too, as far forth as for peace and defence of himself he shall think it necessary, to lay down this right to all things; and be contented with so much liberty against other men as he would allow other men against himself. (p. 87a)

The law of nature, in other words, commands a man to give up his natural liberty (his right to do anything he pleases) for the sake of security. His unlimited liberty does a man little good in the state of nature, since every other man has a similar unlimited right and liberty, so that far from enjoying unlimited rights to everything, every man finds every one of his rights and claims threatened by force or the threat of war. For the sake of peace, then, a man should give up his right to everything, provided only that all other men will likewise give up their rights to everything.

But it is not enough for men to want to give up their natural rights. There must be enforcement of the agreement, so that everyone will keep it. In the state of nature, there can be no guarantee that men, even though they proclaim their intention of living in peace, will actually do so. This is so, even though it is a law of nature that men should live in peace.

For the laws of nature, as *justice, equity, modesty, mercy,* and, in sum, *doing to others as we would be done to,* of themselves, without the terror of some power to cause them to be observed, are contrary to our natural passions, that carry us to partiality, pride, revenge, and the like. And covenants, without the sword, are but words and of no strength to secure a man at all. (p. 99b)

It is not enough for men to agree that they will no longer harm one another. This covenant must be enforced. Some animals, like bees and ants, live naturally in a kind of society. For them, this is a matter of instinct. But for men, it is a matter of

covenant only, which is artificial: and therefore it is no wonder if there be somewhat else required, besides covenant, to make their agreement constant and lasting; which is a common power to keep them in awe and to direct their actions to the common benefit. (p. 100c)

How can such a power come into being as will ensure that men keep their covenants and are able to live in peace? It can only if men

confer all their power and strength upon one man, or upon one assembly of men, that may reduce all their wills, by plurality of voices, unto one will. (p. 100c)

This man or assembly of men is an artificial person. It acts for all those men who together brought it into being. All of them are united in this person as a result of a covenant that every man makes with every man, in this fashion:

I authorise and give up my right of governing myself to this man, or to this assembly of men, on this condition; that thou give up thy right to him, and authorise all his actions in like manner. This done, the multitude so united in one person is called a COMMONWEALTH. (p. 100d)

This person, the commonwealth, since it comes into being for the sake of making a state of peace out of the state of war, may use its strength (which is the strength of the subjects) in any way that it sees fit for the attainment of that end. "And he that carryeth this person," Hobbes concludes his discussion, "is called *sovereign,* and said to have *sovereign power;* and every one besides, his *subject*" (p. 101a).

Let us note several things about the commonwealth. (1) The commonwealth or state is an artificial person. (2) The sovereign is a real person (or assembly of real persons); he (or they) represent the commonwealth. (3) The commonwealth comes to be either by covenant among the subjects or by usurpation and conquest. (4) Its purpose is enforcement of peace among men, through fear.

IV

What are the consequences of this unique act, the social contract, whereby the commonwealth or Leviathan comes into being? We are especially interested in the question of *rights.* With regard to this subject, there are two questions: (1) What are the rights of the state or of the sovereign? (2) What are the rights of the subjects of a sovereign? The two questions are, of course, closely connected.

Let us first consider what are the rights that the sovereign has against the subjects. According to Hobbes's view of the meaning of "right," this question should be stated as follows: What is the sovereign permitted to do in regard to his subjects?

Hobbes devotes all of Chapter XVIII to this question. He considers here the case in which the sovereignty has been created by a vote of the multitude. In Chapter XX he turns to the case of sovereignty that has been acquired by conquest. But he concludes that the manner in which the sovereign has achieved his status makes no difference to the question of rights. "In sum," he says, "the rights and consequences of both

paternal and despotical dominion are the very same with those
of a sovereign by institution; and for the same reasons"
(p. 111a).

Here are the rights as enumerated in Chapter XVIII: (1) The
subjects cannot, under any conditions, cast off the sovereign
and institute a new one. (2) The sovereign has made no covenant with the subjects; rather they have made covenants
among themselves. The sovereign cannot, therefore, ever be
said to have broken the covenant with his subjects, and they
can never be free from their subjection. (3) When the majority
of men has declared someone to be the sovereign, the minority
must go along. (4) The sovereign can commit no injury against
his subjects. (5) Therefore, the sovereign can never be justly
punished. (6) The sovereign has the right of censorship over
opinions and books. (7) The sovereign's will is the sole source
of the civil law. (8) The sovereign has the judicial power in the
state. (9) The sovereign has the right of making war and peace,
and (10) of choosing his officers, counselors, ministers, etc., in
both peace and war. (11) The sovereign has the right of pun-
ishing and rewarding his subjects, and (12) he has the right of
awarding honors and titles.

If we look back on this list of powers and rights, it is so im-
pressive that we may sum up Hobbes's doctrine by saying that
for him *sovereignty is absolute.* This seems to answer the second question we posed above, namely, what rights do the subjects retain in the commonwealth? If sovereignty is absolute,
can the subjects retain *any* rights?

The answer is that they do retain some rights. These are
few, but they are neverthless fundamental. They are those
rights which the subject does not give away, because he *cannot*
give them away. They are, in other words, inalienable rights.
But whereas the American Declaration of Independence 125
years later lists as among man's inalienable rights those to "life,
liberty and the pursuit of happiness," Hobbes's list is much
less inclusive.

There be some rights which no man can be understood by any words, or
other signs, to have abandoned or transferred. As first a man cannot lay
down the right of resisting them that assault him by force to take away

his life, because he cannot be understood to aim thereby at any good to himself. The same may be said of wounds, and chains, and imprisonment. . . And lastly the motive and end for which this renouncing and transferring of right is introduced is nothing else but the security of a man's person, in his life, and in the means of so preserving life as not to be weary of it. And therefore if a man by words, or other signs, seem to despoil himself of the end for which those signs were intended, he is not to be understood as if he meant it, or that it was his will, but that he was ignorant of how such words and actions were to be interpreted. (p. 87c-d)

Of the three inalienable rights mentioned in the Declaration of Independence, Hobbes acknowledges only the first one. The right to life or of self-preservation is inalienable for him. As for the other two, we have seen already that liberty is quite alienable for Hobbes, being in fact totally alienated from the subjects by the social contract and given to the sovereign. Hobbes is silent on any right to a "pursuit of happiness."

V

Is the state natural or conventional for Hobbes?

This question might also be rephrased thus: How do Hobbes and Aristotle compare on the question of the origin of the state? For it is Aristotle, of course, who held that the state is natural, whereas the *Leviathan* again and again refers to the covenant (or convention) by which the state originates. Hobbes would thus seem to be diametrically opposed to Aristotle.

Nevertheless, if we examine the matter carefully, we will find a wide area of agreement between Hobbes and Aristotle. Both of them, in fact, agree that the state is *both* natural and conventional.

We hardly need document the fact that Aristotle maintains that the state is natural because it arises out of man's needs. In the *Politics*, Book I, Chapter 2, he traces the origin of the state, from the union of husband and wife to the family, to a village, and finally to the state. "The state comes into existence, originating in the bare needs of life, and continuing in existence for the sake of a good life. And therefore, if the earlier forms of society are natural, so is the state" (Vol. 9, p. 446a-b).

But Aristotle recognizes that the state, although natural, does

not simply come into being without the voluntary efforts of
men to institute it. He knows that it does not develop in the
way in which, say, a tree naturally develops. "A social instinct
is implanted in all men by nature," he says, and immediately
adds, "yet he who first founded the state was the greatest of
benefactors" (*ibid.*, p. 446c-d). Aristotle, in other words, envisages a time when the state *first* came into being. Furthermore, the coming-to-be of the state is due to some person,
whom he calls a great benefactor. But if the origin of the state
is due to a man (at least in part), it is at least partly conventional. This differentiates a political society, one instituted or
constituted by men, from the society of bees or ants. Their
"state" is completely natural, existing entirely as a result of
their instinctive impulses and actions.

Now let us look at the other side of the question. Is the state
at least partly natural for Hobbes? Here, too, the answer is not
hard. Hobbes says that it is the first law of *nature* to live in
peace, if possible; and if that is not possible, then to wage war
as advantageously as possible. And it is the second law of nature
to be ready to lay down one's right to everything, if other men
will do likewise, for the sake of peace and security.

Thus the state is natural for Hobbes in the same way that it
is for Aristotle. *It arises out of human need.* Men are commanded by a law of their nature to form a state in order to
preserve life. The state, therefore, serves to protect man's inalienable right to life. We need not substantiate the claim that
the state, as described in the *Leviathan*, is also in part conventional—a voluntary institution or, as Hobbes would say, a
work of art.

Is there any difference, then, between Hobbes and Aristotle?
Certainly the emphasis is different. In the *Politics*, Aristotle
seems anxious to convince his reader again and again that the
state is natural. In the *Leviathan*, Hobbes seems anxious to explain again and again the character of the covenant that brings
the state into being.

This difference in emphasis indicates that Hobbes is concerned with a problem which Aristotle ignores. Hobbes is interested in showing what the legitimate rights of the sovereign

are and how he comes to acquire them. By describing in detail the nature of the covenant—who makes it, what is given, what is gained—Hobbes is able to establish what are, in his view, the legitimate rights of a sovereign and what are the rights of subjects. The *Leviathan* could perhaps be characterized as an attempt to show why absolute power on the part of the sovereign is legitimate and so not only must be, but ought to be, borne.

The legitimacy of sovereign power is apparently no problem for Aristotle. Since the state is natural and man needs to live in the state, it is right and good for the state to do all those things which are necessary to accomplish the end for the sake of which it arose, namely, "the good life."

Could the state of nature be conceived differently from the way in which Hobbes describes it?

This question might also be rephrased in the following manner: How do Hobbes and Locke agree and differ in their descriptions of the state of nature? Locke's treatise *Concerning Civil Government*, in which he states his view of the state of nature, was the Eleventh Reading in the Reading Plan, *An Introduction to the Great Books*.

In the second chapter, Locke tells us that the state of nature is

a state of perfect freedom to order . . . actions, and dispose of their possessions and persons as [men] think fit, within the bounds of the law of Nature, without asking leave or depending upon the will of any other man. (Vol. 35, p. 25d)

Does this agree with Hobbes's view? Does Hobbes make the qualification "within the bounds of the law of Nature"? Is the state of nature also a state of freedom for Hobbes?

Locke goes on to say that the state of nature is "a state also of equality, wherein all the power and jurisdiction is reciprocal" (*ibid.*, p. 25d). Does Hobbes consider all men as equal in the state of nature?

Locke continues a little later as follows:

But though this be a state of liberty, yet it is not a state of licence; though man in that state have an uncontrollable liberty to dispose of his person or possessions, yet he has not liberty to destroy himself, or so much as any creature in his possession, but where some nobler use than its bare preservation calls for it. (*Ibid.*, p. 26b)

Is Hobbes's state of nature a state of licence? Does a man have a right to destroy himself? Does he have a right to destroy a thing or person in his possession?

Locke goes on, immediately after the last quotation, in this fashion:

The state of Nature has a law of Nature to govern it, which obliges every one, and reason, which is that law, teaches all mankind who will but consult it, that being all equal and independent, no one ought to harm another in his life, health, liberty or possessions. (*Ibid.*)

Does Hobbes agree that there is a law of nature in the state of nature? Is "reason" the law of nature? Does the law of nature forbid harming other men?

Who enforces the law of nature? Locke says "the execution of the law of Nature is in that state put into every man's hands" (*ibid.*, p. 26c). Does Hobbes differ from him here? In other words, is every man the judge of breaches of the law of nature and does every man have the right to punish others for such breaches?

Finally, let us note what Locke says about the state of nature and the state of war:

And here we have the plain difference between the state of Nature and the state of war, which however some men have confounded, are as far distant as a state of peace, good will, mutual assistance, and preservation; and a state of enmity, malice, violence and mutual destruction are one from another. (*Ibid.*, p. 29b)

For Hobbes, is the state of nature one of good will and mutual assistance? Are the state of nature and the state of war diametrically opposed for him as they are for Locke?

Are there any conceptions of natural law that differ from Hobbes's?

Just as the previous questions called for a comparison between Hobbes, on the one hand, and Aristotle and Locke on the other, so this question seems to involve a comparison of

Hobbes with Aquinas. The Sixth Reading of this Reading Plan was Aquinas' *Treatise on Law,* much of which is devoted to the problem of natural law.

What is the natural law, or the law of nature according to Aquinas? Leaving out the question of who makes law and the problem of its promulgation, Aquinas tells us that a law (any law—including natural law) is "an ordinance of reason for the common good" (Vol. 20, p. 208a). But Hobbes also tells us that "a *law of nature, lex naturalis,* is a precept, or general rule, found out by reason . . ." (p. 86c).

What are the precepts of the natural law according to these two authors? For Hobbes, they are very simple. Let us look at the rest of the passage quoted above:

A *law of nature, lex naturalis,* is a precept, or general rule, found out by reason, by which a man is forbidden to do that which is destructive of his life, or taketh away the means of preserving the same, and to omit that by which he thinketh it may be best preserved. (p. 86c)

Does this differentiate Hobbes from Aquinas? When enumerating the several precepts of the natural law, Aquinas tells us:

In man there is first of all an inclination to good in accordance with the nature which he has in common with all substances; that is, every substance seeks the preservation of its own being, according to its nature. And by reason of this inclination, whatever is a means of preserving human life and of warding off its obstacles belongs to the natural law. (Vol. 20, p. 222c)

Can we find any difference between the two authors on the natural law? They do have different views on what falls under the natural law. For Hobbes, as the quotation shows, every natural law is ordered to the preservation of life. Although Aquinas certainly acknowledges that the natural law commands man (and every other substance) to preserve his life, it also commands many other things. The *first* precept of the natural law is "that good is to be pursued and done, and evil is to be avoided. All other precepts of the natural law are based upon this, so that whatever the practical reason naturally apprehends as man's good belongs to the precepts of the natural law" (Vol. 20, p. 222c).

Thus man is commanded by the natural law not only to

preserve his life (in common with all other substances), but also (in common with all other animals) to engage in "sexual intercourse, education of offspring and so forth." And finally, because man has reason "man has a natural inclination to know the truth about God, and to live in society. And in this respect, whatever pertains to this inclination belongs to the natural law" (*ibid.*, p. 222d). Hence, we see that, for Aquinas, the natural law is ordered to many things beyond the mere preservation of life; in short, its precepts are directed to man's happiness. None of this is present in Hobbes.

What is Hobbes's view of justice?

Here the author with whom we must compare Hobbes is Plato. For the conception of justice that Hobbes advocates is strongly presented in the *Republic*, not as Socrates' view but as that of Thrasymachus. (See the Second Reading in *An Introduction to the Great Books.*)

Let us first consider Hobbes. The third law of nature, he says, is *"that men perform their covenants made."* Then he goes on as follows:

And in this law of nature consisteth the fountain and original of *justice*. For where no covenant hath preceded, there hath no right been transferred, and every man has right to everything; and consequently, no action can be unjust. But when a covenant is made, then to break it is *unjust*: and the definition of *injustice* is no other than *the not performance of covenant*. And whatsoever is not unjust is just. (p. 91a)

But Hobbes goes even beyond this. There can be no valid covenants, he says, until there is some coercive power that compels both parties to a covenant to perform what they have agreed upon. Only such a coercive power can assure that each party to the contract receives his own (*i.e.*, what Hobbes calls his "propriety"). "And therefore," he goes on,

where there is no *own*, that is, no propriety, there is no injustice; and where there is no coercive power erected, that is, where there is no Commonwealth, there is no propriety, all men having right to all things: therefore where there is no Commonwealth, there nothing is unjust. So that the nature of justice consisteth in keeping of valid covenants, but the validity of covenants begins not but with the constitution of a civil power sufficient to compel men to keep them. (p. 91b)

Justice, therefore, comes into being with the state. Until a state exists with laws that determine what belongs to each person, there can be no justice or injustice. But if actions are to be judged just or unjust in terms of whether or not they accord with a law made by the state (a positive law), then how can we judge whether a law is just or unjust?

The answer must be that there is no such thing as an unjust positive law. Even a law that violates a law of nature (for instance, a law commanding us not to preserve our lives) would not be unjust, although it would not be enforceable. Both obedience and disobedience to this law would make a man liable to death.

According to Hobbes, then, there is no positive law, no matter how oppressive, that can be called just or unjust. The appellations "just" and "unjust" are meaningless when applied to laws. They apply only to the actions of subjects, and there they are applied according as the actions conform, or do not conform, to what the law commands. An immediate consequence of this position is that the sovereign, who makes the positive law, cannot do anything that is unjust. Furthermore, since he makes the law, he is above it; there is no law which can compel obedience from him. This, of course, goes along with the fact, pointed out earlier, that the sovereign has right entirely on his side, as well as might, in respect to his subjects. Everything is permitted to him (by right), and nothing is forbidden to him (by law).

Let us briefly recall Thrasymachus' position in Book I of the *Republic*. "I proclaim," he says, near the beginning of his discourse, "that justice is nothing else than the interest of the stronger" (Vol. 7, p. 301b-c). When asked to explain his position by Socrates, Thrasymachus quickly indicates that the "stronger" which he has in mind is the sovereign or government, just as Hobbes. "The government is the ruling power in each state," he declares and continues:

the different forms of government make laws democratical, aristocratical, tyrannical, with a view to their several interests; and these laws, which are made by them for their own interests, are the justice which they deliver to their subjects, and him who transgresses them they punish as a breaker of the law, and unjust. And that is what I mean when I say that in all states there is the same principle of justice, which is the interest of the government; and as the government must be supposed to have power, the only reasonable conclusion is, that everywhere there is one principle of justice, which is the interest of the stronger. (Vol. 7, p. 301c-d)

Clearly this is the same position as Hobbes's: whatever the government or sovereign decides is to its interest and embodies in a law, that is just. There is no standard, for either Thrasymachus or Hobbes, by which governments or sovereigns can be judged.

Was Socrates able to refute the position taken by Thrasymachus? You may wish to reread that section of the *Republic*, for if Thrasymachus is refuted, then so is Hobbes. And it would seem very important to succeed in refuting this portion of Hobbes's argument. If Hobbes and Thrasymachus are correct, we cannot ever say that any government-sanctioned action is unjust. For example, we would have to say that the actions of the Nazi government in Germany were not reprehensible.

Just as the actions of the Nazis would have to be considered just, so the actions of the U.S.S.R. no matter how much we might dislike them, would be not subject to censure by us. Again, we would have to hold that the Nuremberg war-crimes trials were unjust, since the defendants acted in accord with *their* governments' laws. The whole notion of international law, in other words, would have to be thrown out. The only way in which there could be a law of nations, for Hobbes, would be to have a sovereign power over all nations, that is, to have a complete and strong world government. This would involve the surrender of national sovereignty.

The following questions are designed to help you test the
thoroughness of your reading. Each question is to be answered
by giving a page or pages of the reading assignment. Answers
will be found on page 220 of this Reading Plan.

1   What is Hobbes's definition of liberty?

2   Does Hobbes believe in natural slavery?

3   What gives value to things?

4   Is liberty consistent with necessity?

5   Does Hobbes believe in freedom of speech?

6   What is the meaning of *good* and *evil?*

7   Is there any difference between monarchy and tyranny?

8   What are the liberties that a subject has against the
    sovereign?

9   What is the difference between law and right?

10   Does Hobbes think there ever was a real state of nature?

SHAKESPEARE

King Henry the Fourth

Parts I and II

Vol. 26, pp. 434–502

Shakespeare's historical plays are not merely dramatic re-enactments of actual events. They reveal what motivates and what happens to men in the struggle for power. Shakespeare probably never read a line of Machiavelli, but there were Machiavellian currents and Machiavellian figures in the Elizabethan court. He himself created many such figures, full images of flesh and spirit, with an anguished self-awareness.

The present plays could be pure corn, a kind of royal soap opera: "One King's Family." Here is the respectable father, head of the political business, troubled by the scapegrace antics of his eldest son and successor. We have father-and-son talks, scenes of the youthful sowing of wild oats, and a fat-man comedian. A dashing cousin, with get-up-and-go, tries to seize control of the business, but he is foiled. After his father's death the young scamp takes over, turns over a new leaf, and shows he was made of the right stuff all the time.

Using this same plot, Shakespeare gives us human

117

depth and light. Part of this is due to his wonderful language, but with this goes the ability to grasp the inner workings of human character. The respectable old king has a worm gnawing inside of him: his power was gained by rebellion and the degradation and destruction of his predecessor. The fat man is not merely a clown; he is in a strange way the young man's educator, teaching him a side of life and an attitude toward life that he would never learn at home. Commonsensical and cynical-wise, he offers rude dissent to the "for king-and-country" cant of other characters.

For Shakespeare, the people who make history are themselves subject to the perpetual perishing of time, and are keenly aware of how the present moment and their brief lives will be wiped out by the inexorable march of events.

Ninth Reading

I

Although this assignment follows Hobbes's *Leviathan*, Shakespeare was born twenty-four years before Hobbes, in 1564. And the long-lived Hobbes survived Shakespeare's death in 1616 by more than sixty years.

Shakespeare used historical events which took place about 1400 as material for these two plays. Shakespeare is a poet and a dramatist, not a historian. He molds history to suit his dramatic purpose. In Part II of *Henry IV*, for instance, he has the king's death follow almost at once upon the victory over the rebels, whereas in fact eight years elapsed between the two events.

Let us glance at the general historical context in which these plays are set. The main problem of Henry IV was that the legitimacy of his reign was questioned.

The trouble goes back to Henry IV's grandfather, Edward III, who reigned from 1327 to 1377. Edward III's oldest son, also named Edward, was called the Black Prince. The Black Prince died before his father, however, and so the throne went to his son, Richard II, who ruled from 1377 to 1399. Richard's reign was marked by much turbulence and confusion. He was a minor when he ascended the throne, and the time of his minority was one of popular discontent and political strife. After Richard declared himself of age in 1389, there followed a period of constitutional rule and general peace and prosperity. In 1397, however, Richard suddenly and successfully assumed the role of an absolute ruler, crushing the opposition of the parliament and the barons in the process. It was this period of tyranny that paved the way for Henry of Lancaster to become King Henry IV.

Richard had exiled Henry. But in 1399, while the king was in
Ireland suppressing a rebellion there, Henry organized a plot
to overthrow Richard and landed in England. Many of the
barons rallied to his cause. The first of these was the Earl of
Northumberland, as his son Hotspur tells us in Part I:

> My father and my uncle and myself
> Did give him [Henry IV] that same royalty he wears;
> And when he was not six and twenty strong,
> Sick in the world's regard, wretched and low,
> A poor unminded outlaw sneaking home,
> My father gave him welcome to the shore;
> . . . .
> Now when the lords and barons of the realm
> Perceived Northumberland did lean to him,
> The more and less came in with cap and knee;
> Met him in boroughs, cities, villages,
> Attended him on bridges, stood in lanes,
> Laid gifts before him, proffer'd him their oaths,
> Gave him their heirs, as pages follow'd him
> Even at the heels in golden multitudes.
> (Act IV, Scene 3, pp. 459d-460a)

Richard, returning from Ireland, found himself without supporters and was forced to abdicate. Parliament was summoned,
accepted Richard's abdication, and declared Henry of Lancaster to be king of England, as Henry IV, in 1399. (For
Shakespeare's dramatic rendition of Richard's reign, see *King
Richard II*, Vol. 26, pp. 320-351.)

This event is important in English constitutional history because Henry IV owed his crown to Parliament, thus setting a
precedent for the principle that Parliament is superior to the
king. For according to hereditary right, Henry's claim to the
throne was not as good as that of some other claimants.

Richard II was the son of Edward, the Black Prince, who
himself was the oldest son of Edward III. Henry IV was the
son of John of Gaunt, Duke of Lancaster, who was the fourth
son of Edward III. Thus Richard and Henry were cousins. The
second son of Edward III was William, who had already died
in 1336; the third son was Lionel, Duke of Clarence. This
Lionel had a daughter, Philippa, who married the Earl of
March. Her descendants, the House of March, were descended

directly from the third son of Edward III and thus had a better claim to the throne than Henry of Lancaster, who was descended from the fourth son of Edward III. Sir Edmund Mortimer, who appears in the play, belonged to the House of March.

The following table may help to make these relationships clear:

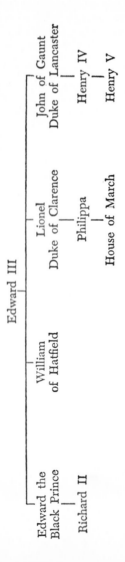

There is reference in Part II of *Henry IV* to the fact that Henry owed his kingdom to Parliament rather than to hereditary right. The Archbishop of York, in defending the rebellion against the king, speaks thus:

> The commonwealth is sick of their own choice;
> Their over-greedy love hath surfeited:
> An habitation giddy and unsure
> Hath he that buildeth on the vulgar heart.
> O thou fond many, with what loud applause
> Didst thou beat heaven with blessing Bolingbroke,
> Before he was what thou wouldst have him be!
> And being now trimm'd in thine own desires,
> Thou, beastly feeder, art so full of him
> That thou provokest thyself to cast him up.
> So, so, thou common dog, didst thou disgorge
> Thy glutton bosom of the royal Richard;
> And now thou wouldst eat thy dead vomit up,
> And howl'st to find it.
> (Act I, Scene 3, p. 473d)

Here, finally, are the dates of the events that bear on the two plays. Richard's abdication and Henry's ascension to the throne took place in 1399. Richard died a few months later; he was probably put to death at Henry's command. (See *King Richard II*, pp. 350d-351a). The battle of Shrewsbury, in which Henry Hotspur died, occurred in 1403; the second rebellion, described in Part II, occurred in 1405. Henry IV died in 1413 and was succeeded by his son, Henry Monmouth, the Prince of Wales, the "Hal" of the plays, who became Henry V.

II

Shakespeare's plays are not political treatises. We cannot consider the *Henry IV* plays as expositions of political theories. They are primarily dramas, to be acted out on the stage. However, these plays deal with important political problems and shed some light on them. Since our interest in this Reading Plan is political, we shall concentrate on their political meaning, leaving it for the most part to the reader to deal with the plays as histories or tragedies, or both.

There are two problems which run throughout the two plays that are of universal interest and importance for political philosophy. The *first* is the question of the legitimacy of a king, or any ruler; the *second* is the question of how to educate a prince or ruler. We have met both of these problems before. Let us begin with the first one.

We have already pointed out that Henry's claim to the throne was, by hereditary right, not as good as that of the descendants of the third son of Edward III.

Evidently Henry IV himself, that is, Shakespeare's Henry IV, felt that his title to the crown was weak. Just before his death, speaking to his son, he says:

> God knows, my son,
> By what by-paths and indirect crook'd ways
> I met this crown; and I myself know well
> How troublesome it sat upon my head.
> . . . .
> . . . . It seem'd in me
> But as an honour snatch'd with boisterous hand
> And I had many living to upbraid
> My gain of it by their assistances;
> Which daily grew to quarrel and to bloodshed,
> Wounding supposed peace: all these bold fears
> Thou see'st with peril I have answered;
> For all my reign hath been but as a scene
> Acting that argument. . .
> (Part II, Act IV, Scene 5, p. 496b-c)

Yet was not his title to the throne strong, in that it had been confirmed by Parliament? England was not at that time a constitutional monarchy, but was in the process of becoming one. One of the factors in that process was the gradual increase in the power of Parliament, until finally it reached the point, in the twentieth century, where Parliament had all the power and the king none.

We discussed another step on this road to parliamentary supremacy in the guide to Locke's *Treatise on Civil Government* in the Reading Plan, *A General Introduction to the Great Books.* We saw that Locke upheld the doctrine that kings govern with the consent of the governed, rather than by divine right. This obviously is a greater inroad on the king's power than the doctrine that his title has to be confirmed by Parliament.

How would Hobbes have viewed Henry's worries concerning the legitimacy of his kingship? Suppose Henry IV had usurped the crown, rather than gained it legitimately (whether by hereditary right or parliamentary grant). In Hobbes's view this would make no difference whatever to the king's rights. Whoever holds the sovereign power has all the rights that go with such power, according to Hobbes. As long as Henry was in fact the sovereign, that is, as long as he had the power of the throne, there could be no legitimate claim against him. In Hobbes's view, the rebellion of the Percies and their allies was certainly not legitimate. Indeed, no rebellion could be legitimate.

However, the problem becomes a little more complicated if we take into account the fact that Henry obtained the crown by rebellion against the legitimate king, Richard II. Could Hobbes countenance that rebellion? Again the answer is No. Henry's rebellion was illegitimate, that is, he had no *right* to rebel. When, however, he had succeeded in making himself king, that very act of usurpation made him the legitimate king, and then there was no longer any right to rebel against him. Hobbes, in other words, is always on the side of the ruling power and condemns all rebellion—always mindful of the fact that a state of war is a state of misery.

Curiously enough, therefore, we find that Henry IV's claim to kingship would be upheld on the one side by a champion of absolutism, such as Hobbes, and on the other side, by a champion of parliamentary rule. Only those who insist on hereditary succession could quarrel with his title.

III

The second problem of these plays concerns the education of Prince Hal for his royal office. The education of a prince is an ever recurring problem. It has been treated or described in many political treatises and biographies. The qualities of a prince or ruler and how they should be developed are discussed in Plato's *Republic*, Aristotle's *Politics*, Plutarch's *Lives* (see, for instance, Plutarch's account of Alexander's education),

Tacitus' *Histories* (we recall the unsuccessful tutelage of Nero by Seneca), Machiavelli's *Prince,* and other works.

The problem of princely education has become less important in modern times. A similar and related problem replaces it. In a government by the many or by all it is necessary to educate everyone, so that each citizen will be able to assume the responsibilities of political action. The problem is still that of educating the rulers, but the rulers in modern industrial democracies are the people.

No one person seems to be in charge of Prince Hal's education, unless we call Falstaff the prince's tutor. It is the King and Hal himself who are concerned with what the prince is learning. Despite his strong disapproval of Hal's way of life and of his companions, the King is unable or unwilling to interfere in Hal's education. In the very first scene of Part I, the King clearly states his discontent with his son, and his wish that he would be more like Harry Hotspur (Henry Percy). When the Earl of Westmoreland praises Hotspur, the King adds:

> Yea, there thou makest me sad and makest me sin
> In envy that my Lord Northumberland
> Should be the father to so blest a son,
> A son who is the theme of Honour's tongue;
> Amongst a grove, the very straightest plant;
> Who is sweet Fortune's minion and her pride:
> Whilst I, by looking on the praise of him,
> See riot and dishonour stain the brow
> Of my young Harry. O that it could be proved
> That some night-tripping fairy had exchanged
> In cradle-clothes our children where they lay,
> And call'd mine Percy, his Plantagenet!
> (Act I, Scene 1, p. 435b)

Prince Hal himself is aware of how unfavorably he compares with Harry Hotspur. Shortly before the battle of Shrewsbury, addressing Hotspur's uncle, he praises Percy:

> The prince of Wales doth join with all the world
> In praise of Henry Percy: by my hopes,
> This present enterprise set off his head,
> I do not think a braver gentleman,
> More active-valiant or more valiant-young,

More daring or more bold, is now alive
To grace this latter age with noble deeds.
For my part, I may speak it to my shame,
I have a truant been to chivalry . . .
(Act V, Scene 1, p. 461d)

The Prince is also aware of his father's disapproval of his conduct. In Act III, Scene 2, of Part I, there is a dialogue in which the King exhorts Hal to change his ways and to be more like the King in his youth, or more like Hotspur, who now threatens to take the crown from Henry IV, just as Henry IV had taken it from Richard a few years before. None of this, however, has any effect on Prince Hal. Although he vindicates himself to a certain extent by besting Harry Hotspur in combat at Shrewsbury, we find him behaving just as before, living as riotously as ever.

Why is the Prince so deaf to his father's advice and public opinion? At least a partial answer is given by the Prince himself. At the end of the very first scene in which Falstaff and Poins appear, Hal comments on them in a soliloquy:

I know you all, and will awhile uphold
The unyoked humour of your idleness:
Yet herein will I imitate the sun,
Who doth permit the base contagious clouds
To smother up his beauty from the world,
That, when he please again to be himself,
Being wanted, he may be more wonder'd at,
By breaking through the foul and ugly mists
Of vapours that did seem to strangle him.

He goes on in the same vein, and ends with this promise:

I'll so offend, to make offence a skill;
Redeeming time when men think least I will.
(Act I, Scene 2, p. 437c-d)

And, after Hal becomes king, he makes good this promise to himself and rejects Falstaff when the latter approaches him in a crowd of people and seeks his attention:

I know thee not, old man: fall to thy prayers;
How ill white hairs become a fool and jester!
I have long dream'd of such a kind of man,
So surfeit-swell'd, so old, and so profane;

But, being awaked, I do despise my dream.
Make less thy body hence, and more thy grace;
Leave gormandizing; know the grave doth gape
For thee thrice wider than for other men.
Reply not to me with a fool-born jest:
Presume not that I am the thing I was;
For God doth know, so shall the world perceive,
That I have turn'd away my former self;
So will I those that kept me company.
When thou dost hear I am as I have been,
Approach me, and thou shalt be as thou wast,
The tutor and the feeder of my riots ...
     (Part II, Act V, Scene 5, pp. 501d-502a)

IV

Who is the nobler person, Henry Percy or Henry Monmouth?

These two young men are the principal antagonists of Part I, and Shakespeare clearly intended to contrast them. But the distribution of virtues and defects in them seems pretty even.

Prince Hal (Henry Monmouth) is a wastrel and given to drinking and careless living; on the other hand, the hotness of Hotspur's character, which earned him his nickname, seems like a considerable defect. Not only will he not let his uncle speak, because of his outbursts of passion (see Act I, Scene 3), but the same rashness also leads him to seek battle under unfavorable conditions.

Again, Prince Hal, by his own admission, neglected the arts of chivalry. Against this stands the fact that he conquered Henry Hotspur in personal combat.

Prince Hal seems unmindful of his high position and the responsibilities that go with being Prince of Wales. By contrast, Henry Hotspur has a high sense of honor and of his duties as a knight and baron. Yet it must be admitted that it is Hotspur who is the rebel and Hal who is on the side of king and Parliament.

The judgment between these two will have to be made by the reader in terms of whatever quality he thinks is most important in a man and in a noble.

Was Prince Hal, after he became king, justified in his attitude toward Falstaff?

There is no doubt that Falstaff was not a suitable companion for a king and that when Prince Hal became Henry V he was well advised to dismiss him. Yet can it not also be said that Falstaff was an unsuitable companion for the Prince of Wales and that Prince Hal should not have associated with him before becoming king? No matter how selfish, gross, cowardly, and gluttonous Falstaff is, we cannot help feeling sorry for him when King Henry V so abruptly and publicly tells him that he no longer wishes to have him around.

We have already quoted the lines in which the Prince states his purpose in seeking the companionship of Falstaff and his ilk—in order to seem the nobler when he reforms. Is this a worthy purpose? Is Prince Hal deliberately misleading Falstaff into thinking that he enjoys his company whereas he is really only using him for his own purposes? Is there not something ungenerous and unprincely in using Falstaff in this fashion?

Furthermore, is it safe for him to associate with companions of whose conduct he does not approve? Hal may think that he can escape being one of them, but is it not likely that in the course of years their manner of acting and thinking will rub off on him? Since the formation of character is largely a matter of forming habits, how can Prince Hal be sure that he is not forming some very bad habits that he may not find easy to break? Is there any evidence in the play that he has formed such habits? Is there any validity to his father's judgment that it subtracts from a prince's dignity to be seen too often in public and in common surroundings? Can Prince Hal's purpose justify the neglect of his duties, such as attendance at the King's council?

Why is Shakespeare so concerned with time?

This is probably an unanswerable question, but one that is nevertheless interesting to speculate about. That Shakespeare thought much about time is well known; many of his plays contain allusions to it, and almost all of his sonnets do. Here we merely invite the reader to consider the role that time, and the changes that occur with time, play in these dramas.

In the second scene of the first act, Shakespeare begins to reveal his preoccupation with time. Prince Hal chides Falstaff for being interested in the time of day. Time is no concern of Falstaff's, Hal says. In the light of what later happens to Falstaff, we may of course disagree with the Prince. The passing of time wreaked terrible changes on Falstaff.

In the second part, the Archbishop of York concludes his reflections on the fickleness of the multitude by remarking:

> O thoughts of men accursed!
> Past and to come seems best; things present worst.

And Lord Hastings concludes the scene by saying:

> We are time's subjects, and time bids be gone.
> (Act I, Scene 3, p. 474a)

A little later, the King reflects on the fickleness of men in words that echo the remarks of the rebellious archbishop:

> O God! that one might read the book of fate,
> And see the revolution of the times
> Make mountains level, and the continent,
> Weary of solid firmness, melt itself
> Into the sea! and, other times, to see
> The beachy girdle of the ocean
> Too wide for Neptune's hips; how chances mock,
> And changes fill the cup of alteration
> With divers liquors! O, if this were seen,
> The happiest youth, viewing his progress through,
> What perils past, what crosses to ensue,
> Would shut the book, and sit him down and die.
> (Act III, Scene 1, p. 483b)

In Act IV, Scene 4, when the King is dying and discovers that Prince Hal has put on the crown, thinking the King already dead, the King chides him for his haste, and discourses at some length about the few hours that remain to him and how the course of time will bring about soon enough what Hal is trying to hasten—Hal's accession to the throne.

There are other passages in the plays that are concerned with time. Time and change are clearly of great importance in the life of men and nations. Much of the science of politics concerns the knowledge of what changes can and what changes cannot be expected to occur in a given time.

We conclude with the words of the dying Hotspur, which constitute the most moving statement on time in these plays:

> O, Harry, thou hast robb'd me of my youth!
> I better brook the loss of brittle life
> Than those proud titles thou hast won of me;
> They wound my thoughts worse than thy sword my flesh:
> But thought's the slave of life, and life time's fool;
> And time, that takes survey of all the world,
> Must have a stop.
> (Act V, Scene 4, p. 465a-b)

The following questions are designed to help you test the thoroughness of your reading. Each question is to be answered by giving a page or pages of the reading assignment. Answers will be found on page 220 of this Reading Plan.

1 Who says "Uneasy lies the head that wears a crown"?

2 Why did Hotspur refuse to turn his prisoners over to the King?

3 What similarity does King Henry IV find between himself and Hotspur?

4 What are Falstaff's thoughts on honor?

5 Who says "The better part of valour is discretion"?

6 Does Northumberland participate in the second rebellion?

7 How does the Earl of Westmoreland defend his stratagem to make the rebels surrender?

8 Why does Henry IV think his son will have a less disputed title to the throne than he had?

MONTESQUIEU

The Spirit of Laws

Preface—Book XIII

Vol. 38, pp. xxi–102

Montesquieu opposed Thomas Hobbes on almost every point. He agreed that civil society is necessary to promote peace, order, and industry. But Montesquieu had a passion for liberty, and he detested any form of government which denied it. It is ironic that the Englishman sought a government with absolute power, while the Frenchman, who lived under such a government, looked to England for an example of proper constitutional rule. Montesquieu saw the people as the ultimate source of governmental power. He denied that any delegated holder of power could rule absolutely.

We find in Montesquieu both ancient and modern notions about civil society. Like Plato and Aristotle, he believed that justice is the end of the state. Like Thomas Aquinas, he believed in a natural law that is embodied in the positive law. But he introduced a new note when he emphasized the historical, sociological, and physical variety of the particular situations in which laws and states take form. It is the particular "spirit" of each nation, formed by all these circumstances, which is the basis of their political institutions. This sense of historical particularity, of concrete spiritual forms, distinguishes Montesquieu from his predecessors and marks the emergence of the historical approach in the modern era.

Montesquieu had a direct effect on actual developments in politics and law, as well as on theories about them. His ideas contributed to the outbreak of the French Revolution and the making of basic law for the new French republic. They also played an important role in the drafting of the federal and state constitutions in the United States.

Tenth Reading

I

In the guide to the Eighth Reading (Hobbes's *Leviathan*) we said that modern political thought was initiated by Hobbes. Montesquieu's *The Spirit of Laws* is one of the books appearing in the 200 years following the publication of the *Leviathan* which profoundly influenced and changed the modern scene. The *Leviathan* was published in 1651; Locke's *Treatise on Civil Government*—read in the Reading Plan, *A General Introduction to the Great Books*—followed in 1690. Montesquieu's work appeared in 1748, Rousseau's *Social Contract*—our next reading—in 1762.

The year 1776 saw the proclamation of the Declaration of Independence, while 1789 was the year in which the Constitution of the United States was adopted and the French Revolution began. John Stuart Mill's *On Liberty* and *Representative Government*, both included in the present Reading Plan, were published in 1859 and 1861, respectively. The other two readings in this Plan—Kant's *Science of Right* and Hegel's *Philosophy of Right*—were also published within this same period, but they are not part of the mainstream of British and American political thought.

The works mentioned have left a heritage of theories and concepts that have been assimilated into our everyday political thinking. An obvious example from Montesquieu is the principle of the separation of powers in government. It is written into the United States Constitution; and in Federalist Paper Number 47 James Madison defended the Constitution against the charge that it insufficiently incorporates this principle. His defense included a lengthy quotation from Montesquieu as the generally acknowledged author of the doctrine. In our own day political debate, while endorsing the principle, rarely mentions Montesquieu as the author of it—an indication of how thoroughly Montesquieu's thought pervades the political tradition of the United States.

II

Our first task is to ask what is meant by "the spirit of laws." What did Montesquieu have in mind when he used this phrase as the title of his work?

By speaking of the *spirit* of laws, Montesquieu signifies that he is concerned with law in general, rather than with any particular body of laws. The spirit of laws, it would seem, must be whatever animates laws, gives them life and utility, and makes them function as they should. But let us read what he himself says about his title.

"Law in general," he writes, "is human reason"; and he continues, "the political and civil laws of each nation ought to be only the particular cases in which human reason is applied" (p. 3c). Law, in general, therefore, is the same everywhere and for all men, but particular laws are and must be different everywhere. "They should be adapted," Montesquieu adds,

in such a manner to the people for whom they are framed that it should be a great chance if those of one nation suit another. (p. 3c)

What are the various factors to which the laws of a country must be adapted? Montesquieu offers the following enumeration of them: "the nature and principle of each government," "the climate of each country," "the quality of its soil," "its situation and extent," "the principal occupation of the natives," "the degree of liberty which the constitution will bear," "the religion of the inhabitants . . . their inclinations, riches, numbers, commerce, manners, and customs." He sums up as follows:

In fine, they [the laws] have relations to each other, as also to their origin, to the intent of the legislator, and to the order of things on which they are established; in all of which different lights they ought to be considered.

This is what I have undertaken to perform in the following work.

These relations I shall examine, since all these together constitute what I call the *Spirit of Laws*. (p. 3d)

Montesquieu's work, therefore, is not a treatise on law as such (as, for instance, Aquinas' *Treatise on Law* is). Instead, we might call it a treatise on how laws ought to be adapted to particular circumstances and situations. A glance at the Table of Contents will show that Montesquieu deals with laws in relation to all the diverse conditions that he has enumerated. This accounts for the length of the work, as well as for some of its repetitiousness. In the thirteen books which constitute our assignment, Montesquieu writes of laws in general (Book I), of laws in relation to the different kinds of government (Books II-VIII), of laws in relation to defensive and offensive force (Books IX-X), and of laws in relation to liberty (Books XI-XIII).

III

One of the most important factors influencing the character of the laws to be found in a country is the kind of government which obtains there. There are, according to Montesquieu, three main kinds of government: republic, monarchy, and despotism.

In order to discover their nature, it is sufficient to recollect the common notion, which supposes three definitions, or rather three facts: that a republican government is that in which the body, or only a part of the people, is possessed of the supreme power; monarchy, that in which a single person governs by fixed and established laws; a despotic government, that in which a single person directs everything by his own will and caprice. (p. 4a)

We must add at once that Montesquieu further distinguishes between two kinds of republics according to whether the whole people or only a part of the people rules. If the whole people rules, the republic is a democracy; if only a part, then the republic is an aristocracy.

While these definitions are unobjectionable, they do not clearly reveal what is important and novel about Montesquieu's classification of the kinds of government. Many writers on political subjects, before and after Montesquieu, have been satisfied to classify the kinds of government according to an accidental principle, namely, the number of persons that rule. Thus we find passages in Hobbes, Locke, and in Aristotle that distinguish governments according to whether one, some, or all rule.

Montesquieu goes beyond the mere number of those who rule to investigate the kind of rule. He begins by distinguishing between the *nature* and the *principle* of a government:

There is this difference between the nature and principle of government, that the former is that by which it is constituted, the latter that by which it is made to act. One is its particular structure, and the other the human passions which set it in motion. (p. 9a)

He adds in a footnote that this distinction is very important. From it, he says, "I shall draw many consequences; for it is the key of an infinite number of laws."

The main division of governments, in terms of their principles, is between despotism, on the one hand, and the other kinds of government on the other. Despotism is *lawless* government; in it "a single person directs everything by his own will and caprice," and its principle is fear:

As virtue is necessary in a republic, and in a monarchy honour, so fear is necessary in a despotic government: with regard to virtue, there is no occasion for it, and honour would be extremely dangerous. (p. 12b-c)

Monarchies and republics are *lawful* governments. This is easily seen in the case of a republic or constitutional government; the constitution is the supreme law in such a government, whether the constitution be democratic or aristocratic.

The monarchies of which Montesquieu speaks are, of course, absolute monarchies (limited monarchies are republics). Nevertheless, an absolute monarchy, unlike despotism, is a lawful government, for as Montesquieu has already told us, in a monarchy "a single person governs by fixed and established laws." Though the monarch is himself the lawgiver and, as such, is not himself subject to the law, his rule is by law and not by caprice.

Having divided governments into lawless and lawful, Montesquieu then divides lawful governments into monarchies and republics, according to their *principles.* "There is no great share of probity necessary to support a monarchical or despotic government," Montesquieu writes. "The force of laws in one, and the prince's arm in the other, are sufficient to direct and maintain the whole. But," he concludes, "in a popular state, one spring more is necessary, namely, virtue" (p. 9b). After saying this, Montesquieu at once launches into historical confirmation of his point, without telling us in detail what he means by "virtue" here. Evidently, he later felt that this was a serious lack, for in the advertisement to the book (presumably written *after* the book was finished) he writes:

What I distinguish by the name of *virtue,* in a republic, is the love of one's country, that is, the love of equality. It is not a moral, nor a Christian, but a political *virtue;* and it is the spring which sets the republican government in motion, as honour is the spring which gives motion to monarchy. Hence it is that I have distinguished the love of one's country, and of equality, by the appellation of political virtue. (p. xxiib)

The principle of republican governments is virtue, therefore; while the principle of monarchical government is honor.

Finally, Montesquieu divides republican governments into democracies and aristocracies. Virtue is the principle of both; but the two forms of republic differ in the extent to which they embody this principle. In a democracy everybody needs to be virtuous; *i.e.,* must love his country and desire equality. Only if this is true can a democratic country be happy and prosperous. Without the love of country and the love of equality, selfish factions will become dominant and democracy will be replaced by despotism. The selfish faction will rule the rest of the population by fear.

Virtue is less necessary in an aristocracy than in a democracy, says Montesquieu (see p. 10c-d). Those who do not belong to the ruling class do not need it so much, since they are ruled by laws and not by their own virtue. However, the ruling nobility must be virtuous, otherwise they will become despotic. What aristocracy needs, therefore, is either eminent virtue in the nobles, or "an inferior virtue, which puts them at least upon a level with one another, and upon this their preservation depends."

Moderation is therefore the very soul of this government; a moderation, I mean, founded on virtue, not that which proceeds from indolence and pusillanimity. (p. 10d-11a)

Montesquieu places great emphasis on republican virtue, the love of one's country and its laws. "As such love requires a constant preference of public to private interest, it is the source of all private virtues; for they are nothing more than this very preference itself" (p. 15d). He points out that this virtue is not acquired by knowledge and that it is a feeling. It is

a sensation that may be felt by the meanest as well as by the highest person in the state. When the common people adopt good maxims, they adhere to them more steadily than those whom we call gentlemen. It is very rarely that corruption commences with the former: nay, they frequently derive from their imperfect light a stronger attachment to the established laws and customs.

The love of our country is conducive to a purity of morals, and the latter is again conducive to the former. The less we are able to satisfy our private passions, the more we abandon ourselves to those of a general nature. (pp. 18d-19a)

This view of political virtue makes democracy seem like a very feasible kind of government, not merely an impractical dream. We must remember that in 1748 there were no democracies actually in existence; the English constitution came nearer to being democratic than any other government, and it was still primarily aristocratic.

IV

What other ways are there of classifying the kinds of government in an essential fashion besides Montesquieu's?

We have already mentioned that many authors classify the kinds of government simply according to the number of those who rule. Although Aristotle in certain passages of the *Politics* adopts this classification, he also can be seen to have another classificatory scheme in mind. This scheme is different from Montesquieu's, but it, too, classifies governments in an essential rather than accidental fashion.

Aristotle's major division is between constitutional and non-constitutional governments. Constitutional governments are those in which the law is supreme; they are governments by law, whereas nonconstitutional governments are governments by person. Sometimes these kinds of government are called political and nonpolitical, respectively.

We must notice how this division differs from Montesquieu's. At first the dichotomy constitutional–nonconstitutional seems to be the same as lawful–unlawful. However, there is an important difference: all constitutional governments acknowledge the constitution or the body of laws as the supreme authority in the state. Not all lawful governments, in Montesquieu's sense, acknowledge this. For instance, in a monarchy—although a lawful government—the king, and not the law, is supreme. The king is above the law. Monarchy is, however, a lawful government, because the king rules *by* law, that is, according to rules laid down by himself. Only if the sovereign rules according to no law or rule, but simply according to caprice, does the government become unlawful, that is, a despotism.

Not all nonconstitutional government (or government by person) need be unjust, according to Aristotle. In some situations, for some subjects, it is appropriate. The father rules over the children, and the master over the (natural) slaves with a rule that is royal or despotic in character, and this rule is just in Aristotle's eyes. The justice is due to the fact that the subjects —the children or slaves—are unable to rule themselves and the fact that the father or master rules these subjects for their own good. But nonconstitutional government that is not directed to the good of the subjects is unjust and tyrannical.

Aristotle's constitutional governments are mainly two. namely oligarchy and democracy. The principle of oligarchy is wealth; that of democracy, freedom. There is a third constitutional government in Aristotle's classification; he calls it polity and it embodies a mixture of the oligarchical and democratic principles. The ruling class of the polity is the large middle class.

Let us indicate in a diagram Montesquieu's and Aristotle's classification of governments:

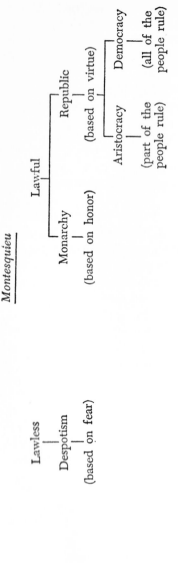

Montesquieu

Lawful
- Monarchy (based on honor)
- Republic (based on virtue)
  - Aristocracy (part of the people rule)
  - Democracy (all of the people rule)

Lawless
- Despotism (based on fear)

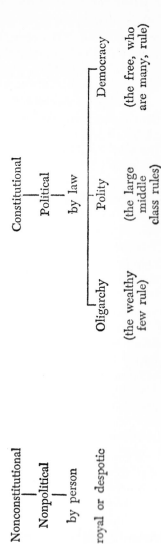

Aristotle

Constitutional
- Political — by law
  - Polity (the large middle class rules)
  - Democracy (the free, who are many, rule)
- Oligarchy (the wealthy few rule)

Nonconstitutional
- Nonpolitical — by person
- royal or despotic

How does excessive equality destroy democracy?

In a democracy there are, Montesquieu says, two excesses to be avoided: "The spirit of inequality, which leads to aristocracy or monarchy, and the spirit of extreme equality, which leads to despotic power, as the latter is completed by conquest" (p. 51d).

It is easy to see how the spirit of inequality might destroy democracy. Inequality is incompatible with the government of all by all and therefore suits only an aristocracy or monarchy. But why should the spirit of extreme equality be dangerous to democracy?

To understand Montesquieu's concern, we must consider such questions as these: In what respect are the citizens of a democracy equal? Are they equal in all respects, or only in one respect, or in several respects?

Is the qualification for citizenship the same as the qualification for political office? In the United States, for example, anyone is qualified for citizenship who (1) was born in the United States, or (2) has been naturalized. Are all United States citizens eligible for all political offices?

Is there any evidence in the Constitution of the United States that it contains aristocratic as well as democratic aspects? If so, would the United States still be a republic (in Montesquieu's sense), but not a complete democracy?

Is selection of political officeholders by lot rather than by election related to the question of equality among citizens?

What is the role of liberty in democracies?

We are so accustomed to associate democracy and freedom that it may be somewhat surprising to realize that Montesquieu says nothing about liberty in his definitions of the nature and the principle of democracy. He emphasizes equality rather than liberty. But he recognizes that liberty is generally thought to be the principle of democracy:

Liberty is generally said to reside in republics, and to be banished from monarchies. In fine, as in democracies the people seem to act almost as they please, this sort of government has been deemed the most free, and the power of the people has been confounded with their liberty. (p. 69a)

But this does not satisfy Montesquieu. The people who hold this view have the wrong notion of liberty. "It is true," he concedes,

> that in democracies the people seem to act as they please; but political liberty does not consist in an unlimited freedom. In governments, that is, in societies directed by laws, liberty can consist only in the power of doing what we ought to will, and in not being constrained to do what we ought not to will.
>
> We must have continually present to our minds the difference between independence and liberty. Liberty is a right of doing whatever the laws permit, and if a citizen could do what they forbid he would be no longer possessed of liberty, because all his fellow-citizens would have the same power. (p. 69a-b)

Liberty does not consist in an ability to do as we please. And Montesquieu adds, democracies are not "in their own nature free."

Montesquieu's thought here follows closely that of Aristotle, who writes:

> In democracies of the more extreme type there has arisen a false idea of freedom which is contradictory to the true interests of the state. For two principles are characteristic of democracy, the government of the majority and freedom. Men think that what is just is equal; and that equality is the supremacy of the popular will; and that freedom means the doing what a man likes. In such democracies every one lives as he pleases. . . But this is all wrong; men should not think it slavery to live according to the rule of the constitution; for it is their salvation. (Vol. 9, p. 512c-d)

Two questions arise. *First*, how is the notion that political liberty is *not* an ability to do as we please compatible with the diversity of belief which is encouraged in the democracies? This diversity manifests itself in the existence of many distinct groups—social, political, religious—with distinct aims. If these groups are to flourish, it seems that everyone must be allowed —within broad limits—to do as he pleases, that is, to choose his way of life and thought.

Secondly, we must ask what political liberty is, if it is not an ability to do as one pleases. Montesquieu gives us a definition of political liberty in Book XII:

> Political liberty consists in security, or, at least, in the opinion that we enjoy security.

The next paragraph makes a little clearer what he means by security:

This security is never more dangerously attacked than in public or private accusations. It is, therefore, on the goodness of criminal laws that the liberty of the subject principally depends. (p. 85a)

The security that Montesquieu has in mind, in other words, is the security of the citizen from arbitrary laws or actions. This becomes clearer when we consider the rest of Book XII. In Chapter 3, Montesquieu points out that laws which condemn a man to death on the testimony of one man "are fatal to liberty." In Chapter 4, he maintains that liberty is favored by laws which fit the punishment to the crime.

There are then no arbitrary decisions; the punishment does not flow from the capriciousness of the legislator, but from the very nature of the thing; and man uses no violence to man. (p. 85c)

Is this also the notion of political liberty in the United States and the British Commonwealth? Do we have provisions to safeguard security, in the sense in which Montesquieu understands it?

How does Montesquieu's conception of liberty compare with Locke's? Are they the same or different?

How does Montesquieu conceive the separation of powers?

The separation of powers consists in the fact that the executive, legislative, and judicial branches of government each have distinct and clearly defined powers. These powers are vested in different persons and one person cannot wield simultaneously both executive and judicial functions, or both legislative and judicial functions, etc. In the United States, it is often charged that one branch of the government usurps powers and functions reserved for the others. Thus, it has been charged that the president often makes laws by administrative decree. Congress has been accused of usurping the judicial function, especially through its committees. The courts, too, have been criticized; in the school integration decision, many people see a usurpation of lawmaking by the Supreme Court.

Any encroachment of one branch of government on the other is a matter of concern, for Montesquieu very clearly states that the purpose of the separation of powers is the preservation of liberty:

The political liberty of the subject is a tranquillity of mind arising from the opinion each person has of his safety. In order to have this liberty, it is requisite the government be so constituted as one man need not be afraid of another. (p. 70a)

In addition to being conducive to liberty, is there any respect in which the separation of powers is inimical to liberty? For example, might not a judiciary that is completely separate from the executive and legislative branches become autocratic? When Franklin D. Roosevelt tried to "pack" the United States Supreme Court in 1938, was this an attack on the principle of separation of powers, or was it a blow for liberty that was being threatened by "nine old men"?

Aside from the question of liberty, are there any arguments that can be made *against* the separation of powers?

The following questions are designed to help you test the thoroughness of your reading. Each question is to be answered by giving a page or pages of the reading assignment. Answers will be found on page 220 of this Reading Plan.

1 What size is appropriate for a republic, a monarchy, and a despotism?

2 Do men and states have a natural right of war?

3 What kind of suffrage is proper to democracy and what kind to aristocracy?

4 Should the ballot be secret?

5 Do severe punishments deter men from committing crimes?

6 Does Montesquieu think that representatives should only act on instructions from their constituents?

7 Where should taxes be heavier, in countries that have liberty or in countries that do not?

8 Which form of government especially requires education?

ROUSSEAU

The Social Contract

Books I–II

Vol. 38, pp. 387–406

Also, L O C K E

Concerning Civil Government [Second Essay]

Vol. 35, pp. 25–81

For a discussion of this assignment,
see the Eleventh Reading in

A General Introduction to the Great Books

M an is born free; and everywhere he is in chains."
This ringing declaration, with which Rousseau opens
The Social Contract, challenges us at once, but leaves
us perplexed as to its truth. In what sense is man born
free? Is it the case that men are everywhere in chains?
Only when we have the answers to these questions are
we prepared to understand Rousseau's solution of the
problem of freedom under government.

The human infant is not free at birth. Freedom, in
Rousseau's view, is something that is acquired. But
what every man is born with, as a matter of innate

endowment, is the right to be politically free. The first part of Rousseau's statement asserts every man's natural right to political liberty—an assertion that is later echoed by the American Declaration of Independence and the French Declaration of the Rights of Man and of the Citizen.

The second part of his statement is intended to describe the political condition of men who, in his century and in most of the preceding centuries, were subject to the despotic power of absolute monarchs. Governed without their consent and having no voice in their own government, they bore the chains of slavery. To be subject to the arbitrary will of rulers who ruled by might alone is, according to Rousseau, to be a slave.

What must be done to emancipate men from slavery or subjection? Rousseau's answer to this question involves two of the most revolutionary ideas in political history, though we have grown so accustomed to them that we fail to recognize their revolutionary character. They are the ideas of republican government and of citizenship.

The only legitimate government, according to Rousseau, is that of a republic, constituted by law and consisting in a government by law rather than by men. The only men who enjoy political liberty under government are the citizens of a republic, each of whom shares in the sovereignty of the government of which he is a constituent as well as a citizen. Rousseau's theory of the social contract has other implications and consequences, but whatever else it means, it heralded the formation of the French and American republics and the birth of freedom through government of, by, and for the people.

Eleventh Reading

I

In the last assignment we discussed the close relation between Montesquieu's theories and the political practices of the English-speaking countries. *The Spirit of Laws,* we saw, frequently draws its examples from the English constitution. But the influence is not all in one direction. The Constitution of the United States, for example, reflects principles set forth in *The Spirit of Laws.* Montesquieu is quoted by James Madison in the *Federalist* as the prime authority on the separation of powers.

Rousseau's ideas also made themselves felt in the American colonies and their influence is discernible in the political thinking of the colonists. But Rousseau's influence was much more dramatically manifested in France. The French Revolution (1789) followed closely on the heels of the publication of *The Social Contract* (in 1762). Rightly or wrongly, Rousseau has been regarded as the intellectual parent of that upheaval.

We shall later face the question of whether *The Social Contract* is in spirit a revolutionary document. From our reading of Montesquieu, we can already see that he is not the author to inspire the French Revolution. The battle cry of the Revolution—liberty, equality, fraternity—does not come from Montesquieu. "Liberty," Montesquieu wrote, "can consist only in the power of doing what we ought to will," not in being able to do whatever we please, which is the kind of freedom that the Revolution fought for. Nor was equality envisaged as an unqualified good by Montesquieu. To be sure, he thought that equality was the principle of democracies, but he also thought that democracies were ruined by an excess of equality. Montesquieu is silent on the question of fraternity.

II

Let us first examine Rousseau's purpose in this book. "I mean to inquire," he tells us, "if, in the civil order, there can be any sure and legitimate rule of administration, men being taken as they are and laws as they might be" (387a-b). He states his purpose again in a famous paragraph at the beginning of the first chapter:

Man is born free; and everywhere he is in chains. One thinks himself the master of others, and still remains a greater slave than they. How did this change come about? I do not know. What can make it legitimate? That question I think I can answer. (p. 387b-c)

Rousseau's aim is to show why and how the enchainment of man is legitimate. This seems a rather curious purpose for a book that is said to have caused a revolution.

To understand Rousseau's meaning, we must investigate several ambiguities in the foregoing statement. In what sense is man born free? How is man everywhere in chains? Why is even the man who thinks himself free nevertheless a slave? What are the criteria of legitimacy in the case of governments?

Like Locke and Hobbes before him, Rousseau employs the conception of a state of nature as a basic term in his political thinking. He is aware of the views of his predecessors on this subject:

The philosophers, who have inquired into the foundations of society, have all felt the necessity of going back to a state of nature; but not one of them has got there. (p. 333c)

This passage does not come from *The Social Contract* but from another work of Rousseau's entitled *A Dissertation on the Origin and Foundation of the Inequality of Mankind.*

When Rousseau says that philosophers have not "got to" the state of nature, he means that they have not been able to find a single historic example of men living in a state of nature. But this, says Rousseau, is irrelevant. We must begin

by laying facts aside, as they do not affect the question. The investigations we may enter into . . . must not be considered as historical truths, but only as mere conditional and hypothetical reasonings, rather calculated to explain the nature of things, than to ascertain their actual origin:

just like the hypotheses which our physicists daily form respecting the formation of the world. (pp. 333d-334a)

For Rousseau the state of nature is a hypothesis which throws light on the present condition of man. That present actual condition is one of enchainment as contrasted with freedom in a hypothetical state of nature. Does this hypothesis help us to explain the legitimacy of the enchainment?

In Chapter 3 of Book I, Rousseau refers to the "right of the strongest." According to Rousseau, the strongest has no right, but only might on his side. But, he adds, "I fail to see what moral effect it can have." The so-called "right of the strongest" lasts only as long as their strength endures.

What kind of right is that which perishes when force fails? If we must obey perforce, there is no need to obey because we ought; and if we are not forced to obey, we are under no obligation to do so. Clearly, the word "right" adds nothing to force: in this connection, it means absolutely nothing. (pp. 388d-389a)

Accordingly, Rousseau concludes this chapter with the declaration:

Let us then admit that force does not create right, and that we are obliged to obey only legitimate powers. In that case, my original question recurs. (p. 389a)

That original question was, "What can make [man's enchainment] legitimate?"

To bring Rousseau's problem into focus even more sharply, let us briefly go back to Hobbes and his account of the origin of civil society. Hobbes, too, starts with the state of nature. But for Hobbes the state of nature is not purely an explanatory hypothesis. He regards it as an actual condition in which mankind once was and some men still are. Men remove themselves from the state of nature (a miserable condition, according to Hobbes) by surrendering all their rights to a sovereign. No question of legitimacy is raised. The sovereign is stronger than any individual in the state and accordingly rules by right as well as by force. Whether the sovereign gains his power as the result of the voluntary submission of men or as the result of naked force makes no difference in Hobbes's eyes. For him, might definitely makes right. All *de facto* rulers rule legitimately. The transition from a state of nature to civil society does not explain the legitimacy of civil government, but, as Hobbes describes it, it throws light on why men are willing to leave the state of nature at any price, including the price of living under absolute rulers or tyrants.

Hobbes agrees with Rousseau that men are everywhere in chains. But the question that Hobbes undertakes to answer is: Why should men be willing to live in chains? Hobbes's answer is simply that living in chains is preferable to living in a state of nature. Rousseau's question and answer are completely different from Hobbes's. Indeed there are many passages in *The Social Contract* which are, explicitly or implicitly, criticisms of Hobbes.

III

Like Hobbes, Rousseau agrees that the state of nature cannot long endure:

I suppose men to have reached the point at which the obstacles in the way of their preservation in the state of nature show their power of resistance to be greater than the resources at the disposal of each individual for his maintenance in that state. That primitive condition can then subsist no longer; and the human race would perish unless it changed its manner of existence. (p. 391b)

The solution of these difficulties lies in the association of men to form a civil society under civil government. But note how complicated the problem becomes for Rousseau because—unlike Hobbes—he wants men to live under government and also to be free:

The problem is to find a form of association which will defend and protect with the whole common force the person and goods of each associate, and in which each, while uniting himself with all, may still obey himself alone, and remain as free as before. (p. 391c)

The solution of this seemingly insoluble problem is to be found in the social contract:

Each of us puts his person and all his power in common under the supreme direction of the general will, and, in our corporate capacity, we receive each member as an indivisible part of the whole. (p. 392a)

In trying to understand this solution, we realize that Rousseau began by posing one problem (the legitimacy of man's enchainment), but ended by solving another (how the members of a civil society can be as free as they were in the state of nature). What causes Rousseau to switch from the first problem to the second? How are they related?

The chains of which Rousseau speaks at the beginning of *The Social Contract* are the chains put on man by the state and by its laws. He might have written this opening sentence by saying "Man is born free, but everywhere he lives under governments." If Rousseau can show, by the terms of the social contract, that to live in civil society under government is *not* to live in chains—because each man "while uniting himself with all, may still obey himself alone, and remain as free as before"—then the solution of the second problem will also provide the solution of the first. The enchainment turns out to be only apparent, and is legitimate to the extent that it places men in a condition of liberty, not servitude.

But how does Rousseau make good his claim that the social contract enables man to be free in civil society because he obeys himself alone? Rousseau's argument hinges on two points. The first, and less controversial, point is this: man gives up natural freedom to gain civil freedom.

Though man is necessarily free in a state of nature, and can be free in a civil society, his freedom is not the same in these two conditions. Man gives up one kind of freedom to gain another.

What man loses by the social contract is his natural liberty and an unlimited right to everything he tries to get and succeeds in getting; what he gains is civil liberty and the proprietorship of all he possesses. If we are to avoid mistake in weighing one against the other, we must clearly distinguish natural liberty, which is bounded only by the strength of the individual, from civil liberty, which is limited by the general will. . . (p. 393c)

This point is not original with Rousseau; we find it in Hobbes and Locke. Rousseau's novel contribution lies in his second point: man in civil society obeys himself alone.

On the face of it, this does not seem to be the case. Citizens are often forced by government or laws to do things against their will. How can a citizen be understood as obeying himself alone when he is forced to act against his will?

> In order then that the social compact may not be an empty formula, it tacitly includes the undertaking, which alone can give force to the rest, that whoever refuses to obey the general will shall be compelled to do so by the whole body. This means nothing less than that he will be forced to be free; for this is the condition which, by giving each citizen to his country, secures him against all personal dependence. (p. 393a-b)

This reveals the crucial point in Rousseau's theory: *men can be forced to be free*. Their enchainment—when it results from a state set up by the social contract—does not lead to slavery but to liberty. For although there are many things that a citizen may be forced to do, nevertheless, if he is forced in a certain way, he remains free.

This doctrine seems quite implausible. But it may have some plausibility if we accept Rousseau's understanding of the social contract, civil society, and, especially, the "general will." In the following section, we shall ask some questions about these basic notions.

IV

What is the general will?

The general will is the will of the state, which, for Rousseau as much as for Hobbes, is to be regarded as an artificial person. When he tells us what the social contract is, Rousseau says that each person puts himself under the direction of the general will. Apart from the state, there is no general will.

But this description of the general will needs to be supplemented by detailed answers to some further questions. How, in fact, is the general will expressed? How does anyone know what the general will wills? By what special quality can the general will elicit obedience from the particular wills of citizens without making slaves of them?

The general will "considers only the common interest"; therefore, it is "always right and tends to the public advantage" (p. 396b). The general will is not the will of all, for this, Rousseau says, is no more than the sum of particular wills.

Since particular wills are directed to particular interests, the will of all is simply the sum of all wills directed to particular interests. But the general will regards the general or *public* interest.

How is the general will on any particular subject determined? By voting and majority opinion, Rousseau says. Each man voting expresses his particular interest, but, in the final result, these divergent particular interests tend to cancel each other, and the pure general will remains. The main difficulty in determining the general will, therefore, arises from the existence of factions. Through factions, the particular wills of this or that group of men become crystallized and no longer cancel one another out. The true general will then becomes obscured (see p. 396b-d).

Does this account of the general will satisfy you? Does it seem as though the majority vote can really determine the general will in Rousseau's sense? Why is what the majority vote determines not simply the will of all? Or, worse yet, the will of most people?

How is a man free when the will of the majority forces him to do something that is contrary to his own particular will?

In Book IV of *The Social Contract*, Rousseau faces this very question. Here is his answer:

I retort that the question is wrongly put. The citizen gives his consent to all the laws, including those which are passed in spite of his opposition, and even those which punish him when he dares to break any of them. The constant will of all the members of the State is the general will; by virtue of it they are citizens and free. When in the popular assembly a law is proposed, what the people is asked is not exactly whether it approves or rejects the proposal, but whether it is in conformity with the general will, which is their will. Each man, in giving his vote, states his opinion on that point; and the general will is found by counting votes. When therefore the opinion that is contrary to my own prevails, this proves neither more nor less than that I was mistaken, and that what I thought to be the general will was not so. If my particular opinion had carried the day I should have achieved the opposite of what was my will; and it is in that case that I should not have been free. (p. 426c-d)

Does Rousseau's theory of the social contract require him to consider one form of government better than another?

The crucial point of the social contract is that it establishes the general will. Any government is legitimate in which the general will prevails. But how is the general will expressed? In laws. And how are laws established? Through majority vote in the assembly of citizens. Any government, therefore, in which this assembly legislates is legitimate, and no other kind is. But a government in which the assembly of citizens rules is a republican, or constitutional, government. *The Social Contract*, therefore, requires legitimate governments to be republican (see p. 400a).

But "republican government" is an even wider term for Rousseau than it was for Montesquieu. As long as the citizens make the laws, it is possible for the actual administration of the government to be given over to all or most of the people (in which case the government is a democracy), or it may be given to a small selected number of people (aristocracy), or it may be given to only one man (monarchy).

There has been at all times much dispute concerning the best form of government, without consideration of the fact that each is in some cases the best, and in others the worst. (Book III, p. 410c)

It is especially worth noticing that Rousseau, though dedicated to the cause of republican government, is by no means an advocate of democracy.

If we take the term [democracy] in the strict sense, there never has been a real democracy, and there never will be. It is against the natural order for the many to govern and the few to be governed. It is unimaginable that the people should remain continually assembled to devote their time to public affairs, and it is clear that they cannot set up commissions for that purpose without the form of administration being changed. (p. 411a)

And a little later he adds:

there is no government so subject to civil wars and intestine agitations as democratic or popular government, because there is none which has so strong and continual a tendency to change to another form, or which demands more vigilance and courage for its maintenance as it is. . .

Were there a people of gods, their government would be democratic. So perfect a government is not for men. (p. 411b-c)

What is Rousseau's theory of law?

Rousseau gives us a capsule definition of law:

When the whole people decrees for the whole people, it is considering only itself; and if a relation is then formed, it is between two aspects of the entire object, without there being any division of the whole. In that case the matter about which the decree is made is, like the decreeing will, general. This act is what I call a law. (p. 399c-d)

How does this definition of law compare with Aquinas' definition of law? Aquinas' definition, you may remember (see the guide to the Sixth Reading), has four parts noting that a law has to be (1) a thing of reason, (2) made by him who has care of the community, (3) for the common good, and (4) properly promulgated. Does Rousseau's definition cover these same points? If not, which one does he omit?

Some of the answers to these questions are contained in the following paragraph that follows shortly after the definition of law:

It can no longer be asked whose business it is to make laws, since they are acts of the general will; nor whether the prince is above the law, since he is a member of the State; nor whether the law can be unjust, since no one is unjust to himself; nor how we can be both free and subject to the laws, since they are but registers of our wills. (pp. 399d-400a)

Rousseau's theory of law has, however, another important feature. That is the conception of the *legislator*. By this, Rousseau does not mean the man or men whose business it is to make the ordinary laws for the state, such as legislators in Congress or Parliament. Rather, he intends by the "legislator" the person who laid down the fundamental law of the state prior to its existence. He has in mind such mythical figures as Lycurgus or Solon. The extraordinary thing about the legislator is this: his establishing the form or constitution of the state is necessary before the state can come into being; yet, because there is not yet any state, his actions have no authority except what they derive from himself.

Thus in the task of legislation we find together two things which appear to be incompatible: an enterprise too difficult for human powers, and, for its execution, an authority that is no authority. (p. 401c)

Have there ever been any real legislators, or are they always mythical figures like Lycurgus and Solon? Since the state of nature is only hypothetical, the legislator is also, of course, only hypothetical. However, within a few years of *The Social Contract*'s publication the revolutions in America and France resulted in the deliberate establishment of constitutions. The Constituent Assembly in France and the Constitutional Convention in America undertook the task of Rousseau's legislator. The American Constitutional Convention, for instance, created the basic law for a nation which did not yet exist.

Finally, it is worth noting that constituent assemblies, to perform the task of Rousseau's legislator, did not end with the American Convention. The various revolutions of 1848 gave rise to new constitutional assemblies; the German republic after World War I was worked out in an assembly at the city of Weimar; and the Charter of the United Nations was shaped and discussed at the congress of nations in San Francisco in 1945.

The following questions are designed to help you test the thoroughness of your reading. Each question is to be answered by giving a page or pages of the reading assignment. Answers will be found on page 221 of this Reading Plan.

1 Are there slaves by nature?

2 Is the social contract agreed upon by majority vote?

3 What is an act of sovereignty?

4 What are the two ends of laws?

5 In Rousseau's view are all men equal?

6 Is it possible to renounce liberty altogether?

7 In passing from the state of nature to the civil state, man gives up his natural liberty and gains civil liberty. In addition, Rousseau says, he gains a third liberty. What is it?

8 What are the kinds of law?

KANT

The Science of Right

Introduction and Second Part

Vol. 42, pp. 397–402, 435–458

On any subject the writings of Immanuel Kant have certain distinctive qualities. His books have an elaborate and intricate architecture, but he is always painstakingly clear about the system of his thought. He acquaints the reader in advance with the major divisions and subdivisions of any subject that he is treating, and he always proceeds from part to part in accordance with an order of discussion which he has carefully laid out. The paragraphs are like so many signposts which keep the reader apprised of the successive stages in the development of the exposition or argument.

Another characteristic of Kant's style reflects the method of his thought. He always proceeds from principles to their consequences and always tries to show how the consequences follow from the principles. He enunciates the principles themselves in the most abstract and universal terms, so that they are applicable to the widest variety of concrete and particular facts.

The terms in which the principles are stated are de-fined by Kant with precision and clarity. The careful reader is never left in doubt as to the meaning of the fundamental propositions; nor is he left in doubt with regard to the grounds on which Kant advances them. Step by step, everything is reasoned as rigorously as possible.

Such system, order, and precision may be expected in metaphysics or mathematics, but it is unusual in the field of political theory. The reader will find here the familiar notions of constitutional government and citizenship, of political rights and duties, of the forms and powers of government, of freedom, justice, and equality—notions he has met in the writings of other authors included in this Reading Plan. But they are transformed by the method with which Kant treats them, and the reader will enrich his understanding of them by re-examining them in the new light that is thrown on them by Kant's definitions, his universal principles, and the rational connections between them which are made explicit by Kant's systematically reasoned exposition.

Twelfth Reading

I

The Science of Right is a late work of Kant's; it was published in 1797. His three major critiques all precede it—the *Critique of Pure Reason* (1781), the *Critique of Practical Reason* (1788), and the *Critique of Judgement* (1790). *The Science of Right* is part of a larger work, the *Metaphysic of Ethics,* some other parts of which are also included in Volume 42. In treating the philosophy of law as an integral part of moral philosophy, Kant follows in the footsteps of many of his predecessors. Aquinas, for instance, places his *Treatise on Law* in that part of the *Summa Theologica* which deals with moral problems.

The selection assigned consists of the Introduction and the Second Part, which is entitled "Public Right." The First Part, entitled "Private Right," is not included in this reading.

II

Let us begin with a quick survey of the political doctrine stated in this book. Kant's political theory does not differ significantly in content from that of his predecessors—such as Hobbes, Locke, Montesquieu, and especially Rousseau.

Kant describes the origin of civil society in terms of a state of nature and a social contract. The state of nature is a nonjuridical state, Kant says; that is, a state in which there is no distributive justice, rendering to each his due. By contrast, the civil state is a juridical state in which distributive justice obtains.

Kant's view of the state of nature is more moderate than Hobbes's. Nevertheless, he remarks that in such a condition everyone would do what seems good only to him. Like Rousseau and Locke, Kant describes the state of nature as a state of freedom, but a freedom that is precarious and insecure. Men give up this freedom to enter civil society and in so doing gain a different and better freedom.

With Locke, Kant considers the legislative power as the most important function of the state, to be exercised by none but the people. While Kant's "united will of the people" is reminiscent of Rousseau's "general will," we do not find in Kant, either explicitly or implicitly, the notion of a man's being forced to be free.

Kant follows Montesquieu's view of the powers of government and of their separation. Like Rousseau, Kant is dedicated to the proposition that all legitimate government is republican in character. *The Science of Right* offers much support for the view that Kant was deeply influenced by Rousseau, especially in his moral philosophy.

What, then, is new or distinctive about Kant's political theory? First of all, his account of the transition from a state of nature to civil society is an original contribution. Hobbes, Locke, and Rousseau all offer a basically utilitarian statement of the reasons that might have persuaded men to make this change. These three authors differ in their descriptions of the state of nature, and they differ in their views of what man gains by forming a civil state. But they all justify the transition by the result: what is gained (whether it be security, moral freedom, or civil liberty) is greater or better than what is given up (the independence men enjoyed in a state of nature).

Kant clearly is not unaware of the dangers and violence inherent in the state of nature. But his argument, explaining why men depart from a state of nature to enter into civil society, does not take account of these utilitarian considerations. On the contrary, his reasoning here is completely in line with his moral reasoning elsewhere: what men should do is a matter of duty and moral imperatives, not a matter of ends to be achieved. He writes:

But it may be said of the *juridical* state that: "All men who *may* even involuntarily come into relations of right with one another *ought* to enter into this state." (p. 434a)

And again a litttle later he speaks of the *postulate* of public right, where we may assume that he is using the word "postulate" in its root meaning of "demand":

From the conditions of private right in the natural state, there arises the postulate of public right. It may be thus expressed: "In the relation of unavoidable coexistence with others, thou shalt pass from the state of nature into a juridical union constituted under the condition of a distributive justice." (p. 434b)

Kant's posture, in other words, is that of a moralist. He maintains that men *ought* to pass into the juridical state simply because it is wrong to live in the lawless state of nature. Men who "live and continue in this state of externally lawless freedom" are, he says, "in the highest state of wrong, as being and willing to be in a condition which is not juridical" (p. 434c).

Kant's condemnation of the state of nature—as not merely harmful but actually wrong—is reiterated, perhaps even more strongly, when he considers nations as existing in a state of nature in relation to one another. He tells us that

the natural state of nations as well as of individual men is a state which it is a duty to pass out of, in order to enter into a legal state. (p. 455c)

This duty, like all duties, derives from the command of pure practical reason:

the morally practical reason utters within us its irrevocable veto: *There shall be no war*. So there ought to be no war, neither between me and you in the condition of nature, nor between us as members of states which, although internally in a condition of law, are still externally in their relation to each other in a condition of lawlessness; for this is not the way by which any one should prosecute his right. . .

It may be said that the universal and lasting establishment of peace constitutes not merely a part, but the whole final purpose and end of the science of right as viewed within the limits of reason. . . (p. 457b-d)

The view that it is a moral duty for men to seek peace and to form a state is strikingly different from the views of other authors who are concerned with the transition from state of nature to civil society. Hobbes does not consider war or the state of nature wrong, only dangerous. Locke sees nothing immoral in the state of nature which, for him, is not lawless but has the law of nature to govern it. Rousseau urges men to form a civil society for utilitarian reasons.

Kant's moral condemnation of the state of nature and the warfare which results from it is most explicit when he considers not men, but nations, in a state of nature. In *Perpetual Peace* (New York, 1939), a little work which echoes much of the *Science of Right*, Kant's concluding words are about the duty to abolish war between nations:

If it is a duty, if the hope can even be conceived, of realizing, though by an endless progress, the reign of public right—perpetual peace, which will succeed to the suspensions of hostilities, hitherto named treaties of peace, is not then a chimera, but a problem, of which time, probably abridged by the uniformity of the progress of the human mind, promises us the solution. (p. 67)

III

One of the most striking features of *The Science of Right* is its thoroughgoing republicanism. The legislative power must belong to the united will of the people. Those who are united for the purpose of legislating are the citizens, and the citizens enjoy these three juridical attributes:

1. constitutional freedom, as the right of every citizen to have to obey no other law than that to which he has given his consent or approval; 2. civil equality, as the right of the citizen to recognise no one as a superior among the people in relation to himself, except in so far as such a one is as subject to *his* moral power to impose obligations, as that other has power to impose obligations upon him; and 3. political independence, as the right to owe his existence and continuance in society not to the arbitrary will of another, but to his own rights and powers as a member of the commonwealth, and, consequently, the possession of a civil personality, which cannot be represented by any other than himself. (p. 436d)

These three juridical attributes of citizenship can be realized only through a republican form of government. In fact, in *Perpetual Peace*, Kant explicitly affirms this:

The only constitution resulting from the idea of the social compact, upon which every good legislation of a nation ought to be founded, is a republican constitution. It is the only one established upon principles compatible with, first, the liberty of all the members of a society in the quality of men; second, with the submission of all to a common legislation, as subjects; and third, with the right of equality, which all share as members of a state. (pp. 12-13)

Kant's republicanism, however, does not by any means imply that Kant advocates universal suffrage. The notion that all persons—men and women, rich and poor, property owners and the propertyless—are to be enfranchised was almost inconceivable in 1800. Kant, in harmony with his time, maintains that only a limited number of those men living in a state are to be admitted to citizenship, in the sense of having full rights to vote and to hold office.

But Kant makes an important contribution to the theory of citizenship by making a distinction between *active* and *passive* citizenship. What he has to say in this context makes it clear that it is merely the circumstances of life in the eighteenth century which prevent him from favoring universal suffrage, and not any belief in the innate superiority of some men which fits them alone for the office of citizenship.

The *active* citizens are all those who are entitled to vote. All other members of the state are *passive* citizens. These persons, though not entitled to have a voice in their own government, are nevertheless called citizens. We must inquire what quality they share with the active citizens that makes it appropriate to apply the name "citizen" to both.

First, however, let us see who these "passive" citizens are.

The apprentice of a merchant or tradesman, a servant who is not in the employ of the state, a minor . . . all women, and, generally, every one who is compelled to maintain himself not according to his own industry, but as it is arranged by others (the state excepted), are without civil personality, and their existence is only, as it were, incidentally, included in the state. (p. 437a)

Such persons are in Kant's opinion not

qualified to exercise the right of suffrage under the constitution, and to be full citizens of the state, and not mere passive subjects under its protection. For, although they are entitled to demand to be treated by all the other citizens according to laws of natural freedom and equality, as *passive* parts of the state, it does not follow that they ought themselves to have the right to deal with the state as active members of it, to reorganize it, or to take action by way of introducing certain laws. (p. 437b)

The active citizens, in short, are all those who have a measure of independence in the state. All those whose livelihood and existence depend on the will of others are passive citizens, for voting, Kant says, "presupposes the independence or self-sufficiency of the individual citizen among the people, as one who is not a mere incidental part of the commonwealth, but a member of it acting of his own will in community with others" (pp. 436d-437a).

But though the passive citizens are not the equal of the active citizens as members of the state, they are the equal of them *as men*. As men, therefore, they have a right to claim

that whatever be the mode in which the positive laws are enacted, these laws must not be contrary to the natural laws that demand the freedom of all the people and the equality that is conformable thereto; and it must therefore be made possible for them to raise themselves from this passive condition in the state to the condition of active citizenship. (p. 437b-c)

This answers our earlier query, why passive citizens are to be called citizens at all. They are potential citizens, for the state must make it possible for them to change from their dependent status to the independent condition of active citizens. This change would, of course, be largely an economic change. For if everyone residing in a state is to be an active citizen, then no one in that state must be dependent on another's will for his livelihood. The notion that such a condition should be established is, indeed, quite revolutionary, though Kant's way of stating it is very calm and matter of fact.

Here again we can detect the moralist in Kant: it is not right for passive citizens to be kept perpetually in their state of disfranchisement because, *as men*, they are the equals of the active citizens. Hence their condition *must* be changed, and the development of civil society *must* bring this change about.

IV

A striking example of the way in which Kant's political ideas derive from his moral ideas is to be found in his theory of punishment. Treatises on punishment usually distinguish three purposes for which criminals are punished. *First*, there is the retributive or retaliatory purpose. Punishment of this kind restores the balance of justice that has been upset by the crime; it retaliates against the criminal. The Old Testament doctrine of "an eye for an eye, and a tooth for a tooth" is retaliatory in character. *Secondly*, punishment may have a deterrent effect; that is, the punishment of the criminal may deter others from committing similar crimes. *Thirdly*, punishment may be remedial or reformative in character; that is, the punishment may benefit the criminal by making a better and more useful citizen out of him.

Kant is emphatic that punishment must never be anything but retributive.

Juridical punishment can never be administered merely as a means for promoting another good either with regard to the criminal himself or to civil society, but must in all cases be imposed only because the individual on whom it is inflicted *has committed a crime.* (p. 446b)

In this insistence, Kant is a long way from modern penal theories, most of which acknowledge only remedial and deterrent punishment as legitimate. Retribution or retaliation is usually felt to be mere vengeance and, as such, uncivilized. Kant's reasoning in favor of retribution is worthy of our attention. Remedial or deterrent punishment is instituted for the sake of benefiting either the criminal himself or the rest of society. Thus, the criminal is being *used*—though used for a worthy purpose, namely, the diminution of the number of crimes committed. But, Kant maintains, it is wrong for a person to be used, no matter how beneficent the purpose for which he is being used.

One man ought never to be dealt with merely as a means subservient to the purpose of another. . . Against such treatment his inborn personality has a right to protect him. . . He must first be found guilty and *punishable*, before there can be any thought of drawing from his punishment any benefit for himself or his fellow-citizens. (p. 446b-c)

Far from remedial punishment being something that the criminal should welcome, Kant considers that he has a right to be protected from it.

This extends even to capital punishment. The crime of murder requires that the murderer be put to death. On account of his humanity the murderer is entitled to capital punishment. Any lesser punishment treats him as less than a man and more like a thing. Things may be used as means to an end, but to use a man as a means is to treat him like a thing and thus to detract from his dignity. Only capital punishment is commensurate with both the crime of murder and the fact of the murderer's humanity.

The distinction between persons and things is derived from morality. The idea that punishment should not be utilitarian, but should restore the moral balance in the world, is also clearly derived from ethics rather than from a theory of law.

V

What is Kant's conception of right?

The question "What is right?" is, Kant says, "about as embarrassing to the jurist as the well-known question, 'What is truth?' is to the logician." We may take it as evidence of this embarrassment that Kant himself never quite directly answers the question, but talks around it. Nevertheless, we can discern what he means by "right."

Generally speaking, the right and the lawful are the same. This indicates that Kant is using the word "right" in an altogether different way from Hobbes. For Hobbes, "right" and "law" are opposed in roughly the same way that freedom and obligation are opposed. But for Kant "the conception of right [refers] to a corresponding obligation which is the moral aspect of it" (p. 397c).

The closest Kant comes to a definition of right is in the following sentence:

Right, therefore, comprehends the whole of the conditions under which the voluntary actions of any one person can be harmonized in reality with the voluntary actions of every other person, according to a universal law of freedom. (pp. 397d-398a)

And a little later he writes:

Every action is *right* which in itself, or in the maxim on which it proceeds, is such that it can coexist along with the freedom of the will of each and all in action, according to a universal law. (p. 398a)

We have already noted that the area of the right and the lawful are roughly the same. Does this mean that, if we now speak precisely, *right* and *law* are identical? For instance, consider the definition of a law that Aquinas gives in the *Treatise on Law*. Does it fit Kant's conception of right? Who makes rights? Who enforces them? Are there different kinds of rights, just as there are different kinds of law?

What is Kant's division of rights?

Kant divides rights in two different ways (see p. 401b). First, there is the division into *natural* and *positive* right. "Natural right," Kant says, "rests upon pure rational principles *a priori.*" By contrast, positive right "is what proceeds from the will of a legislator." *The Science of Right* is only concerned with natural right. Indeed, there can be no science of positive right, since what comes from the will of a legislator is arbitrary. But there can be a science or knowledge of natural right, since its principles are pure, rational, and a priori, that is, can be known without any appeal to experience.

An obvious example of a positive right may be useful. It is right, in the United States, to drive automobiles on the right side of the road. But this is clearly an arbitrary decision. If it had been decided differently, it could just as well be right to drive on the left side of the road. There can be no theoretical treatment of such arbitrary rights.

The second division is into *innate* and *acquired* rights. "Innate right is that right which belongs to every one by nature," while "acquired right is that right which is founded upon . . . juridical acts." It is clear that all innate rights must fall within the group of natural rights. It would seem that acquired rights might be either natural or positive. Since, however, *The Science of Right* deals only with natural rights, it takes account only of natural acquired rights. Right that is natural *and* acquired is right that is based on pure, rational, a priori principles but requires juridical acts to be brought into being.

Kant tells us that there is but one innate right, the right of freedom. Consequently, it would seem that the entire *Science of Right* is given over to a treatment of natural, acquired rights. And these rights are again divided into *private* and *public* right.

The following questions remain to be answered: What is the right of freedom? What is private right? What is public right? Is Kant's division of rights consistent? Is he correct in holding that there is only one innate right? How do the "inalienable rights" of the Declaration of Independence fit into Kant's scheme of rights?

What are the rights of nations?

Nations are, with respect to one another, in a state of nature and, consequently, in a state of continual war. The rights of nations, therefore, are simply rights with respect to war. Kant distinguishes three areas of right here: the right of going to war, right during war, and right after war. Let us consider the second of these.

The determination of what constitutes right *in* war, is the most difficult problem of the right of nations and international law. It is very difficult even to form a conception of such a right, or to think of any law in this lawless state without falling into a contradiction . . . It must then be just the right to carry on war according to such principles as render it always still possible to pass out of that natural condition of the states in their external relations to each other, and to enter into a condition of right. (p. 454a)

Kant here states an important principle. Nothing must be done, even in war, which would make war the permanent condition of mankind. It must always be possible to re-establish peace between warring nations and the further possibility of perpetual peace between all nations must also be preserved.

From this principle, Kant derives various detailed commands and prohibitions. Wars should not be punitive, nor should a war aim at the extermination of the enemy. With regard to the subjects of the warring nations, several important precepts follow. They must not be ordered to do anything which would make them unfit as citizens. For by destroying them as citizens, the state destroys itself and thus renders peace unattainable.

In general, Kant's view is that the end of war is peace. No means must be employed which contradict that end.

The following questions are designed to help you test the thoroughness of your reading. Each question is to be answered by giving a page or pages of the reading assignment. Answers will be found on page 221 of this Reading Plan.

1 Does Kant think there ever was an actual state of nature?

2 What is the distinction between autocracy and monarchy?

3 What is equity?

4 Is there any right of revolution or dethronement?

5 Does Kant think that the three powers of government ought to be separate?

6 Does a citizen have a right of emigration?

7 Should the sovereign exercise the right of pardon freely?

8 Can anyone make himself a slave by contract?

J. S. MILL

Representative Government

Ch. 1–8

Vol. 43, pp. 327–389

Also, Selections from *The Federalist*

Vol. 43

For a discussion of this assignment,
see the Fourteenth Reading in

A General Introduction to the Great Books

J ohn Stuart Mill's *Representative Government* is the first great work in political theory which argues for the proposition that democracy is the ideal form of government. The central democratic principle of universal suffrage was not only an untried and radical proposal in 1861, but it was also one that aroused justifiable fears of mob rule or, at least, misgovernment by the uneducated and inexperienced mass of working-men. Mill himself shared these fears, and he proposed systems of weighted voting and proportional representation to overcome the tyranny of an underprivileged majority legislating in its own interest when it obtained the franchise. But he had the courage, nevertheless, to defend the principle of universal suffrage on the grounds of justice or right—the right of every man to have a voice in matters which are the common concern of all.

The date 1861 may seem incredibly late for the first great work in political theory to espouse the cause of democracy. Was there no earlier enunciation of the view that every man has a natural right to be a citizen with suffrage?

Yes. In 1647 a group of men in Cromwell's army called the Levellers insisted that every man born in England—the propertyless many as well as the propertied few—had a right to the franchise. And in 1821, in the United States, a similar stand was taken by a group of radicals who advocated reforming the constitution of New York State in the direction of universal suffrage. But in neither case did the spokesmen for extending the franchise even contemplate granting suffrage to women, to slaves, or to Negroes. Mill placed no such reservations on the word "all" when he maintained that all men—all human beings regardless of sex, race, color, or previous condition—should be full-fledged citizens with a voice in their own government.

Not only was Mill the first to expound and defend the theory of democracy, but it is also the case that the theory preceded the practice of democracy. The second and third great reform bills in England, which gradually extended the suffrage to the working classes, came in 1867 and in 1884. The admission of Negroes to citizenship came with the Civil War amendments in the United States. Woman suffrage did not prevail in England or the United States until the twentieth century. And as recently as 1948, President Truman's Commission on Civil Rights found it necessary to argue the case for every man's right to be a citizen and the need to devise practical measures to secure for every man the free and full exercise of the right to vote.

Representative Government was a tract for the times in Mill's day. It is still one in our day, and, considering the world at large, it is likely to be for some time to come a tract for the future.

Thirteenth Reading

I

John Stuart Mill was born in 1806, the oldest son of James Mill. The elder Mill was himself an outstanding philosopher, political thinker, and practical statesman, but in all these categories he was to be surpassed by his son. John Stuart's education was directly under the care of his father who, in John Stuart's words (in the *Autobiography*) "exerted an amount of labour, care and perseverance rarely, if ever, employed for a similar purpose, in endeavouring to give, according to his own conception, the highest order of intellectual education."

James Mill believed in stretching his young son's mind to the utmost. John Stuart began to study Greek and arithmetic at the age of three, Latin at the age of eight. At the age of seven he had read six dialogues of Plato including the *Theaetetus* "which last dialogue, I venture to think," he writes in the *Autobiography*, "would have been better omitted, as it was totally impossible that I should understand it." Before Mill was twelve he had studied Euclid and algebra, the Greek and Latin poets, and some English poetry. He also took a great interest in history, especially ancient history.

The greatest influence on the younger Mill's mind, however, was his association with his father and his father's friends. John Stuart studied political economy while James Mill was working on his *Elements of Political Economy*; he studied law with Austin and economics with Ricardo. He also became a convinced and ardent Benthamite. When Jeremy Bentham and James Mill founded the *Westminster Review* as the organ of Benthamite views and the views of the Philosophical Radicals, John Mill was a major contributor. In the year 1825, he also edited Bentham's *Rationale of Judicial Evidence*.

At the age of twenty, in 1826, Mill suffered what he called "a crisis in my mental history." His youthful energy and enthusiasm waned and he became greatly depressed. "Suppose," he asked himself, "that all your objects in life were realized; that all the changes in institutions and opinions which you are looking forward to, could be completely effected at this very instant: would this be a great joy and happiness to you?" The answer, given by "an irrepressible self-consciousness" was "No." This depression, in its most severe form, lasted several months and altogether it affected Mill for three or four years. He finally emerged from it with a new appreciation for the value of the emotions and a realization that philosophical analysis was only part of human life.

Mill gained experience in governmental practice with the East India Company. Like his father, he worked in the examiner's office of the company and, also like his father, he rose to be chief examiner. Mill spent thirty-five years at India House, retiring in 1858 when the company was dissolved and its functions were taken over by the government. Mill disapproved of the change; in his opinion the interests of both England and India would have been better served if the East India Company had retained its governmental functions. Some of his reasons for thinking so are stated in the last chapter of *Representative Government*.

In 1830, Mill first met Mrs. Harriet Taylor, the wife of John Taylor. Concerning his friendship with Mrs. Taylor, Mill writes that it "has been the honour and chief blessing of my existence, as well as the source of a great part of all that I have attempted to do, or hope to effect hereafter, for human improvement." Mill never ceased to praise Mrs. Taylor's influence on his work and, indeed, maintained that she ought to be considered the co-author of many of his works. "What I owe, even intellectually, to her, is in its detail, almost infinite," he writes. In 1851, two years after the death of her first husband, Mrs. Taylor became his wife, and although during the seven years of their married life Mill published less than at any other period of his career, he thought out and discussed with his wife such important works as *On Liberty* (published in 1859), *Rep-*

resentative Government (1861), and *Utilitarianism* (1863). All these books were published within a short time of Mrs. Mill's death. Though his wife influenced Mill's thought in many respects, we suspect this was especially so on the subject of the equality of women. An article, "The Enfranchisement of Women," was published in the *Westminster Review* in 1851. The essay was generally taken to have been written by John Mill, but actually Mrs. Mill was the author. The article did, however, lay the groundwork for Mill's own work on the subject, *The Subjection of Women,* published in 1869.

Other works of Mill that must at least be mentioned include *A System of Logic* (1843), *Principles of Political Economy* (1848), and *An Examination of Sir William Hamilton's Philosophy* (1865).

Mill died on May 8, 1873, in his cottage in Avignon which had been built so that he might be close to the grave of his wife, who had died at Avignon, on November 3, 1858.

II

Representative Government holds a unique position among the great books on political philosophy. It is the first of such books to expound the modern theory of democracy and it is also the first one to defend this kind of democracy as the best form of government.

How do modern and traditional theories differ in their conception of democracy? Plato and Aristotle were acquainted with forms of government that they called democracies. In their use of the term, a democratic form of government exists when "the many," or "the commons," rule. But we must not be deceived into thinking that the people who rule—though they are many in number and common in status—comprise every adult in the state. Not even every male adult is included in the ruling group. The rulers, therefore, remain a selected group, and this form of government is democratic only by comparison with the kinds of government to which it is opposed, for example, oligarchy and aristocracy. As contrasted with these kinds of government, the suffrage is extended in traditional democracies to more than a few people. Not merely the few who are noble, or the few who are rich, but many —including relatively poor people—rule in these traditional democracies.

But democracy in this sense is still a long way from what Mill understood by the term. To Mill, democracy meant nothing less than universal suffrage. In the democracies that Plato and Aristotle knew or envisaged a great many men (and, of course, all women) had no ruling power. The clearest evidence for this is the compatibility of the traditional view of democracy with a large slave class.

Though Plato and Aristotle differ in their conceptions of democracy, neither favors it. Plato calls it "a charming form of government, full of variety and disorder, and dispensing a sort of equality to equals and unequals alike" (*Republic*, Book VIII, Vol. 7, p. 409d). In his opinion democracy is not only a disorderly form of government, but it also quickly and almost invariably degenerates into tyranny (see Vol. 7, pp. 411d-413a). Aristotle is not quite so unequivocally opposed to democracy. Although at one point he counts it among the bad forms of government, at other times he recognizes that, in terms of what is possible, it is a relatively good form of government, better than oligarchy. But he calls the worst form of democracy that in which the citizens (that is, those entitled to vote) are most numerous. (See *Politics*, Book VI, Ch. 4-5, Vol. 9, pp. 522a-524b.)

By contrast, Mill's endorsement of democracy is unequivocal.

There is no difficulty in showing that the ideally best form of government is that in which the sovereignty, or supreme controlling power in the last resort, is vested in the entire aggregate of the community; every citizen not only having a voice in the exercise of that ultimate sovereignty, but being, at least occasionally, called on to take an actual part in the government, by the personal discharge of some public function, local or general. (p. 344d)

III

What are the reasons that persuaded Mill to take such a favorable view of representative democracy? In the first two chapters, he deals with two preliminary problems, the solution of which will help to answer the main question. In Chapter 1, Mill discusses how far governments, and political matters in general, are subject to human choice. Then, in Chapter 2, Mill examines the criteria by which we judge the goodness of a particular form of government.

With regard to the first problem Mill concludes that men can, to a large extent, do something about their governments. Governments do not simply come into being by accident, nor do they grow in inevitable fashion out of the character and circumstances of a people. Thus Mill denies the views of what he calls the naturalistic school of political thinkers:

> The fundamental political institutions of a people are considered by this school as a sort of organic growth from the nature and life of that people: a product of their habits, instincts, and unconscious wants and desires, scarcely at all of their deliberate purposes. (p. 328b)

Neither, on the other hand, can circumstances and conditions be completely neglected. Not every form of government is possible for every kind of people. Even representative democracy, the best form of government, is not suitable to all peoples. "There are . . . conditions of society," Mill writes in the last chapter, "in which a vigorous despotism is in itself the best mode of government for training the people in what is specifically wanting to render them capable of a higher civilisation" (p. 436b). There are three conditions which must be taken into account when we consider whether a form of government is suitable for a given country:

> The people for whom the form of government is intended must be willing to accept it; or at least not so unwilling as to oppose an insurmountable obstacle to its establishment. They must be willing and able to do what is necessary to keep it standing. And they must be willing and able to do what it requires of them to enable it to fulfil its purposes. (p. 329a)

Mill concludes that

> within the limits set by the three conditions so often adverted to, institutions and forms of government are a matter of choice. (p. 331b)

Turning now to the second preliminary problem, let us see what Mill considers to be the criterion of a good government. It is easy to state that criterion in formal terms. The best gov-

ernment is one which fulfills the purposes for which governments are established. But Mill does not stop here. He considers what the purposes of government are and concludes
that "the merit which any set of political institutions can possess" consists

partly of the degree in which they promote the general mental advancement of the community, including under that phrase advancement in
intellect, in virtue, and in practical activity and efficiency; and partly of
the degree of perfection with which they organise the moral, intellectual,
and active worth already existing, so as to operate with the greatest
effect on public affairs. (p. 338b)

IV

The double criterion given in the last quotation must be
used to show that representative democracy is the best form
of government. Mill must convince us, in other words, (1) that
representative government promotes, to a greater degree than
any other government, "the general mental advancement of
the community," and (2) that it utilizes, in a better fashion
than any other government," the moral, intellectual, and active
worth already existing" in the community. Let us see what
Mill has to say on both of these points.

(1) Mill is quite passionate in his contention that self-government will benefit men because of the influence that it will
have upon the improvement of their character. Here he makes
use of one of his favorite themes (which also plays a prominent
part in *On Liberty*)—the superiority of an active type of
character over a passive one.

The best kind of person, and the happiest, according to
Mill, is one who is not content merely to remain what he is,
but who constantly tries to improve himself. Such a person
will constantly expand his moral and intellectual energies to
find new paths to tread. He will not be content simply to conform to the customs and prejudices of his community, but will
blaze a trail in a new direction. He will always be learning,
and he will be willing to embark on unusual paths of thought
and action for the sake of discovery. Such a person will be an
individualist in the best sense of that word, and he will be
truly free.

This active type of character is greatly encouraged by self-government, whereas other forms of government suppress it in varying degrees. Indeed, for many men, participation in government may be the first step toward liberation from the chains of custom and conformity.

It is not sufficiently considered how little there is in most men's ordinary life to give any largeness either to their conceptions or to their sentiments. Their work is a routine; not a labour of love, but of self-interest in the most elementary form, the satisfaction of daily wants . . . Giving [a person] something to do for the public, supplies, in a measure, all these deficiencies. If circumstances allow the amount of public duty assigned to him to be considerable, it makes him an educated man. (p. 349b)

Not only is the mind of the citizen improved by participation in government, but his moral education is also furthered. The citizen must put aside selfish considerations and consider the common good. He

is called upon . . . to weigh interests not his own; to be guided . . . by another rule than his private partialities; to apply, at every turn, principles and maxims which have for their reason of existence the common good: and he usually finds associated with him in the same work minds more familiarised than his own with these ideas and operations, whose study it will be to supply reasons to his understanding, and stimulation to his feeling for the general interest. He is made to feel himself one of the public, and whatever is for their benefit to be for his benefit (p. 349c-d)

(2) Self-government uses the existing good qualities of a people in the best way, because it promotes the common good by enlisting the energies of all the people. It most efficiently protects the rights and interests of the people, because each person is the best defender of his own rights:

Does Parliament, or almost any of the members composing it, ever for an instant look at any question with the eyes of a working man? When a subject arises in which the labourers as such have an interest, is it regarded from any point of view but that of the employers of labour? I do not say that the working men's view of these questions is in general nearer to the truth than the other: but it is sometimes quite as near; and in any case it ought to be respectfully listened to, instead of being, as it is, not merely turned away from, but ignored. (p. 345d)

All this, of course, merely shows the superiority of democracy over other forms of government. It does not, as such, show that *representative* democracy is the ideal form of government. That follows almost as an afterthought, in the last paragraph of Chapter 3: self-government is best, but direct self-government can function only in a small town. Therefore, representative self-government must be the truly ideal form for large and populous states.

V

What means does Mill propose in order to counteract the "tyranny of the majority"?

The enemies of democracy, from Plato onward, have charged that democracy almost always turns into a kind of tyranny. The majority rules, to be sure, but, in its dealings with the minority, the majority can be as despotic and arbitrary as a single tyrant. A democracy is especially liable to this danger if the ruling majority is unscrupulous, promotes its own factional interests rather than the common good, and has ways of perpetuating its dominant position.

Mill shares this apprehension concerning majority rule:

The pure idea of democracy . . . is the government of the whole people by the whole people, equally represented. Democracy as commonly conceived and hitherto practised is the government of the whole people by a mere majority of the people, exclusively represented. (p. 370b)

The ruling majority is likely to rule in its own interest, and not to regard the interest of the minority. But this is not just, in Mill's opinion.

Nothing is more certain than that the virtual blotting-out of the minority is no necessary or natural consequence of freedom; that, far from having any connection with democracy, it is diametrically opposed to the first principle of democracy, representation in proportion to numbers. It is an essential part of democracy that minorities should be adequately represented. No real democracy, nothing but a false show of democracy, is possible without it. (p. 372b)

We can understand Mill's problem and the general outlines of his proposed solution in terms of an imaginary example drawn from the political scene in the United States. Let us imagine that one of the states has a population of 1,000,000 eligible voters and let us also assume that each of those eligible actually votes. Furthermore, let our imaginary state be represented in the House of Representatives by ten congressmen from exactly equal districts. Each of the congressmen then comes from a district that has 100,000 voters in it.

Suppose there is a congressional election. We will assume that in each congressional district the Democratic candidate wins, and that each of them wins by the identical margin of 60,000 votes to 40,000. In compliance with the United States system of selecting its governing body, our hypothetical state would be represented by ten Democratic congressmen and by no Republicans at all.

This, Mill says, is unjust. For although in each congressional district there was a Democratic majority, nevertheless there were, in the entire state, 400,000 Republican votes. And these 400,000 votes are not represented at all, even though 400,000 is a far larger number than 60,000—60,000 being the size of the majority that elected one congressman.

One remedy for this alleged injustice consists in apportioning the congressmen according to the total number of votes cast in the state. Under such a plan, the ten available seats in the House of Representatives would be divided between Democrats and Republicans in the ratio of six to four. In other words, there would be six Democratic congressmen and four Republican congressmen.

In essence this is Mill's plan—or Mr. Hare's plan, since Mill gives full credit to him as being the author of the proposal. Determination of the number of representatives that a party is to have in a legislative assembly according to the proportion of votes cast for it is called *proportional representation*.

Our hypothetical example shows that representatives to the Congress are not elected according to the method of proportional representation. Presidential elections in the United States are conducted according to a scheme that is the very opposite of proportional representation. If one presidential candidate receives the majority of votes in a state, then he receives *all* the electoral votes of that state, no matter how sizable the minority may be that voted for his opponents. As a result the popular vote for the presidential candidates is always much closer than the electoral vote, since the electoral vote completely disregards the minority votes.

There is something very persuasive in the arguments advanced by Mill and others in favor of proportional representation. It definitely results in a legislative assembly that is a more exact image of the divisions of popular opinion than can otherwise be obtained. And it seems just that the assembly should mirror the country as a whole.

Justice, no matter how important, is not, however, the only consideration that must be taken into account when setting up governmental machinery. A government must also be able to govern efficiently and for this it requires a considerable measure of stability. A good government must strike a balance between the demands of justice and those of stability. It must not let the search for justice paralyze it into inaction; nor must it, for the sake of efficiency and stability, fall into the injustice of dictatorship or tyranny.

Proportional representation seems to encourage unstable governments, though of course it is not the only cause of them. We can illustrate this with an example. Compare the stable governments that exist in the United States and Great Britain with the weak and ever-changing governments in France before and after World War II. Neither the United States nor Great Britain follow the method of proportional representation, whereas the Third and Fourth Republics of France did.

The correlation between proportional representation and unstable governments is more than accidental. For example, the governmental instability in postwar France was in large part due to the numerous parties that were represented in the Legislative Assembly. Many of them had only a few seats in the Assembly and could not hope to accomplish anything positive. Yet together these small splinter parties commanded enough votes so that there either was no majority party at all or else there was a party whose majority was so slim that it could hope to govern only by allying itself with one or more of the other parties. This in turn resulted in compromises and an unwillingness on the part of the government to take strong action even when it was necessary, since each of the various parties was afraid of alienating its much needed allies.

The nonproportional method of voting in the United States and Great Britain tends to maintain only two appreciably strong parties. If a third party in the United States is to be taken seriously, its presidential candidate would probably be expected to receive some electoral votes. Thus he would be required to obtain the majority of all the votes cast in at least one state—a much less likely result than simply getting a small percentage of the popular vote throughout the nation.

We see, then, that proportional representation is not without its drawbacks. Do the disadvantages connected with it outweigh its desirable features? Are there any disadvantages to nonproportional representation? Is there some way of combining these two methods of electing representatives that will take advantage of the good points in each while avoiding the drawbacks of each? Which is more important in matters affecting governmental procedure—justice or efficiency?

Who governs in a representative government?

Mill is perhaps more concerned with the problem of who should *not* govern in a representative government than he is with that of who should govern. *The representative body ought not to govern,* he tells us again and again in Chapter 5, which is entitled "Of the Proper Functions of Representative Bodies."

This position is, in Mill's view, entirely compatible with the conception of representative government.

The meaning of representative government is, that the whole people, or some numerous portion of them, exercise through deputies periodically elected by themselves the ultimate controlling power, which, in every constitution, must reside somewhere. This ultimate power they must possess in all its completeness. (p. 355b-c)

But a little later Mill adds that "there is a radical distinction between controlling the business of government and actually doing it" (p. 356b). By their very nature representative bodies are unfit to administer as one man can decide and act much more ably than a body of men. "The proper duty of a representative assembly in regard to matters of administration is not to decide them by its own vote, but to take care that the persons who have to decide them shall be the proper persons" (p. 358a-b).

What, then, is the proper function of the representative body? "What can be done better by a body than by any individual is deliberation" (p. 357a). Deliberation, and only deliberation, is the proper function of the representative assembly. The representatives must decide whether to approve or disapprove actions proposed by the government in all its branches. In so doing, they maintain the ultimate control of the government.

It is interesting to see that Mill's concern with the separation of these two functions is echoed by a contemporary writer, Walter Lippmann, who writes in *The Public Philosophy* (Boston, 1955):

The executive is the active power in the state, the asking and the proposing power. The representative assembly is the consenting power, the petitioning, the approving and the criticizing, the accepting and the refusing power. The two powers are necessary if there is to be order and freedom. But each must be true to its own nature, each limiting and complementing the other. The government must be able to govern and the citizens must be represented in order that they shall not be oppressed. The health of the system depends upon the relationship of the two powers. If either absorbs or destroys the functions of the other power, the constitution is deranged. (*The Public Philosophy*, p. 30)

Lippmann further thinks that in modern democratic government these two functions have not been kept sufficiently separated:

In the effort to understand the malady of democratic government I have dwelt upon the underlying duality of functions: *governing*, that is, the administration of the laws and the initiative in legislating, and *representing* the living persons who are governed, who must pay, who must work, who must fight and, it may be, die for the acts of the government. I attribute the democratic disaster of the twentieth century to a derangement of these primary functions.

The power of the executive has become enfeebled, often to the verge of impotence, by the pressures of the representative assembly and of mass opinions. (*Ibid.*, pp. 54-55)

If Mill is right, is the representative assembly in the United States (that is, the Congress) functioning properly? Should it have the function of initiating and drafting laws? It is often said that the power of government (meaning the executive arm of the government) has grown tremendously since the 1930's, and that the power of Congress has become proportionally weaker. How is this compatible with Lippmann's view that the power of the executive has been eroded by the encroachment of the representative assembly?

Does Mill think that all men are entitled to suffrage?

Mill's answer is clearly affirmative. Only children, illiterates, and those on public relief are, in his opinion, properly excluded from suffrage. We may assume that he would as a matter of course also exclude convicted criminals.

Mill's advocacy of suffrage for women is in accord with his life and career. We have already seen that he and his wife championed the political equality of men and women. After his wife's death Mill became active in the woman suffrage movement and, during a term in Parliament, worked for the enfranchisement of women. Great Britain was not yet ready to follow Mill's suggestions in this respect, however. A limited franchise was granted to women in 1918, and complete political equality for women did not come until 1928 in Britain. In the United States the nineteenth amendment to the Constitution gave the vote to women in 1920.

We may recall that seventy years earlier Kant, in *The Science of Right*, acknowledged that universal suffrage is an ideal toward which states and constitutions should strive. In his time, however, he believed that a division of citizens into active (voting) and passive (nonvoting) was still entirely proper. In contrast, Mill sees no need to disfranchise anyone.

Kant and Mill differ in what they consider to be the important first step on the road to the enfranchisement of all men. For Kant, suffrage should be granted to persons after they have become independent through education and improved economic status. For Mill, on the other hand, it is suffrage itself which is the greatest educational means for raising mankind to a higher level.

The following passage indicates how important Mill considers suffrage, from the point of view both of utility and of justice:

Whoever, in an otherwise popular government, has no vote, and no prospect of obtaining it, will either be a permanent malcontent, or will feel as one whom the general affairs of society do not concern. . .

It is a personal injustice to withhold from any one, unless for the prevention of greater evils, the ordinary privilege of having his voice reckoned in the disposal of affairs in which he has the same interest as other people. If he is compelled to pay, if he may be compelled to fight, if he is required implicitly to obey, he should be legally entitled to be told what for; to have his consent asked, and his opinion counted at its worth, though not at more than its worth. There ought to be no pariahs in a full-grown and civilised nation; no persons disqualified, except through their own default. (p. 382b)

Should everyone's vote count equally?

Everyone is entitled to vote, but, in Mill's opinion, some men should be able to vote two or three times. Thus some men would have a greater influence than others in deciding the affairs of the state. This right to more than one vote should be based on some just qualification, such as superior education or mental ability. It definitely must not, Mill says, be based on accidental circumstances, such as the possession of property.

This method of voting is called "plural voting." Is it compatible with justice? Is it compatible with Mill's own views concerning universal suffrage and the function of representatives? Are there any dangers in plural voting? How could abuses of this system be avoided? How would mental superiority be determined?

The following questions are designed to help you test the thoroughness of your reading. Each question is to be answered by giving a page or pages of the reading assignment. Answers will be found on page 221 of this Reading Plan.

1 What does Mill mean by progress? by order?

2 What are Mill's arguments against despotism?

3 What conditions would make Communism possible?

4 What counterarguments does Mill advance to the view that women should be deprived of suffrage, since they would vote as dependents?

5 What part of the government should have the power of taxation?

6 Should the representative assembly make laws?

7 Why should taxation be widespread?

8 Which is the most desirable type of human character?

HEGEL

Philosophy of Right

Introduction and Third Part,
Subsection III (The State)

Vol. 46, pp. 9–20, 80–114

Of all the contributions to political theory which are included in this Reading Plan, that of Hegel is least likely to elicit a sympathetic response in a democratic audience. On the contrary, its main tenets are such as to produce an emotional antipathy verging even on an unwillingness to give his views a fair hearing. Yet they deserve our closest attention in spite of the distaste they may arouse in us, precisely because they represent so clearly and powerfully the antithesis of our most fundamental convictions.

It is sometimes said of Hegel's *Philosophy of Right,* as it is also said of Plato's *Republic,* that here is the intellectual source of totalitarianism, whether that takes a Fascist or Communist form. To say this is to caricature serious philosophical doctrines, though it must be admitted that these books, especially if read unsympathetically, lend themselves to such distortion. This is particularly true of Hegel's doctrine that the state is an organic whole of which its human members are but parts, as arms and legs are parts of living organisms. And it is, perhaps, even more strikingly true of Hegel's conception of the state as a being which he does not hesitate to call "divine"—the embodiment on earth of the divine spirit.

These doctrines are, of course, accompanied in Hegel by principles of right and justice, by the highest respect for law as the voice of reason, and by an insistence on constitutional government, all of which sharply distinguishes Hegel's treatment of the state as paramount and even divine from the totalitarian aggrandizement of the state as an overwhelming power, with complete disregard for the reign of law and principles of justice. But while this may help us to see that Hegel is not himself in favor of totalitarianism, the fact remains that he is also not in favor of individualism.

Where believers in democracy hold, as one of their deepest convictions, that the state is made for man, not man for the state, Hegel holds the very opposite. However, his criticisms of individualism are trenchant and penetrating. They challenge us to consider whether individualism cannot be carried to an extreme which is as inimical to sound political ideals as is the opposite extreme of totalitarianism.

Fourteenth Reading

I

Georg Wilhelm Friedrich Hegel (1770-1831) is one of the few philosophers to rival Aristotle in the universality of his interests and in the systematic fashion in which he treats all matters that come under his purview. The works that he published (or that were published from his lecture notes after his death) deal with metaphysics or ontology, theology, psychology, religion, art, logic, law, history, philosophy of nature, philosophy of history, and the history of philosophy.

Hegel constructed a philosophic system. He does not treat the various fields as independent realms, but binds everything together with a few central ideas. It is difficult to understand any part of Hegel's system without understanding the whole.

The *Philosophy of Right,* though definitely part of the Hegelian system, nevertheless can be more easily read separately than some of Hegel's other works, since it has its roots in matters that are familiar to us from other writers. It deals with law, with freedom, and with right, with the state, and with the individual's relation to the state.

To make this reading assignment a little easier, let us consider two things that are central in Hegel's philosophy. The first has to do with the content of his philosophy, the second with his philosophical method.

(1) Hegel is often called an "idealist" in philosophy, or even an "absolute idealist." His idealism consists in the fact that for Hegel what is most real are ideas, or concepts, or thoughts. The most important aspect of the world is its ideal or rational structure. The sensible or phenomenal aspect of the world (what we see, hear, feel, etc.) is intelligible only insofar as we recognize it as partaking of rationality. Thought, concept, or

spirit rules the world, and sensible appearances must be understood as embodiments of these. We would do well to remember this when, in the *Philosophy of Right*, we read about the state and its institutions. These are of interest to Hegel only insofar as they reflect the rational spirit which is reality. For Hegel, the real is the ideal.

(2) Hegel calls his method "dialectical." Since reason or spirit is the central idea of his philosophy, much of it may be considered a "dialectic of spirit." The dialectical approach, in Hegel's sense, involves viewing everything, including ideas, as developing and changing. Most important is the development that occurs when an idea and its opposite clash. Out of such a meeting of a "thesis" and its "antithesis" there emerges a "synthesis"—a stage of development in which the earlier opposites are both contained, but in such a fashion that they are reconciled. In the *Philosophy of Right*, we have a clear instance of this in Hegel's treatment of the state, which is a synthesis of two opposite poles, subjective and objective freedom.

A few remarks are in order about Hegel's importance in the history of thought. His philosophy had enormous influence on the English thinkers of the latter half of the nineteenth century. For many years, Hegelian idealism ruled the British schools of philosophy. More important than his success in England, however, is Hegel's influence on Karl Marx and on Marxists. Marxism has taken from Hegel the notion of "dialectic" as the only proper philosophical method. Marxism, however, believes not in a dialectic of spirit, but rather, since it affirms only material substances as real, in a "dialectical materialism." Dialectical materialism borrows from Hegel the view of the inevitable conflict between opposites. The resolution or synthesis incorporates everything that was important in the original opposites, but in a higher and more significant way.

II

A glance at our previous readings in this Plan suffices to convince us that freedom is a major theme in modern political writing. The subject of freedom usually arises in connection with the question of how much power the state should have and how many rights the citizen or subject should have or retain. This is the way freedom is treated, for example, by such writers as Hobbes, Locke, Rousseau, and Kant.

In contrast, ancient and medieval political writings seem to neglect the topic of freedom. In such writers as Plato, Aristotle, and Aquinas the major theme is not how much power the state has, but rather to what end the power of the state is to be used. "What is the end of the state?" is the main political question in these writers. Since the seventeenth century, however, that question has been replaced by Rousseau's: "Man is born free; yet everywhere he is in chains. What is the reason for this and what makes it legitimate?"

Hegel presents a curious mixture of these two traditions. Like his contemporaries and immediate predecessors, he is very much concerned with the problem of freedom. At the same time, Hegel comes on the tradition of the ancients in that what ultimately decides all political questions for him is the nature and purpose of the state. Nothing is right, in Hegel's view of things, which does not serve the state. Yet the supremacy of the state is perfectly compatible with the demands of freedom, for the end of the state is freedom.

The conceptions of the state and freedom do not mean the same thing to Hegel as they do to most other political writers. Let us investigate Hegel's use of these key terms a little more closely.

"The state is the actuality of concrete freedom" (Sec. 260, p. 82a). There can hardly be a more direct and absolute identification of the state with freedom. In what sense is "freedom" being used here? Hegel not only identifies the state with freedom, he also tells us (p. 80b) that "the state is absolutely rational." Taking these two statements together, we guess that for Hegel freedom and rationality are closely related, and are perhaps even identical. We do not have far to look for confirmation of this guess.

Rationality, taken generally and in the abstract consists in the thoroughgoing unity of the universal and the single. Rationality, concrete in the state, consists (*a*) so far as its content is concerned, in the unity of objective freedom (i.e. freedom of the universal or substantial will) and subjective freedom (i.e. freedom of everyone in his knowing and in his volition of particular ends); and consequently, (b) so far as its form is concerned, in self-determining action on laws and principles which are thoughts and so universal. (p. 80c-d)

Subjective freedom is the freedom of an individual person. It is the freedom of that individual to be himself, to act and do as he and he alone pleases. For most political writers this kind of freedom is one of the highest political goods, if not *the* highest. They often say that the purpose of the state consists in preserving as much of this freedom as possible. Some of this freedom, they say, may have to be sacrificed in the state, but that which remains is much more secure than it was in the state of nature.

For Hegel, however, subjective freedom is far from being a desirable thing. Objective freedom is the real freedom. It is the freedom which the will achieves when it wills, not what it pleases, but what is right for it. The object of the will when it thus wills rightly is necessarily universal.

Subjective freedom, for Hegel, is mere arbitrariness. There is nothing good or rational about a man's ability to choose either this way or that way. It is much better and much more rational for a man to be determined by what is objectively, universally, and necessarily good. A man so determined in his choices and actions will not be free in the sense of subjective freedom: he will no longer be able to choose. But he will be free in the objective sense: he will be free from all those attractions that the will ought *not* to follow because they are not truly good for man.

The idea which people most commonly have of freedom is that it is arbitrariness—the mean, chosen by abstract reflection, between the will wholly determined by natural impulses, and the will free absolutely. If we hear it said that the definition of freedom is ability to do what we please, such an idea can only be taken to reveal an utter immaturity of thought, for it contains not even an inkling of the absolutely free will, of right, ethical life, and so forth. (p. 16a)

This kind of freedom is of a low order because, in order to exercise it, the will is still dependent on something outside itself, namely, the alternatives between which it chooses. By contrast, the truly free will is free just because it is free *from* any outside influence. It is completely independent because it is entirely self-dependent.

Only in freedom of this kind is the will by itself without qualification, because then it is related to nothing except itself and so is released from every tie of dependence on anything else. The will is then true, or rather truth itself. . .

The will is then universal, because all restriction and all particular individuality have been absorbed within it. (p. 17d)

Finally, Hegel, in summing up his conceptions of the subjective and the objective will, summarizes his views on subjective and objective freedom:

The subjective, in relation to the will in general, means the will's self-conscious side, its individuality . . . in distinction from its implicit concept.

But

the will is purely and simply objective in so far as it has itself for its determination and so is in correspondence with its concept and genuinely a will. (p. 18a-b)

We now return to the statement which we quoted earlier, that "the state is the actuality of concrete freedom." What remains to be seen is how the state can be the embodiment of freedom. Here the freedom that Hegel has in mind is, of course, the true, or objective, freedom. He continues, after the above sentence, as follows:

But concrete freedom consists in this, that personal individuality and its particular interests not only achieve their complete development . . . but, for one thing, they also pass over of their own accord into the interest of the universal, and, for another thing, they know and will the universal; they even recognize it as their own substantive mind; they take it as their end and aim and are active in its pursuit. The result is that the universal does not prevail or achieve completion except along with particular interests and through the co-operation of particular knowing and willing; and individuals likewise do not live as private persons for their own ends alone, but in the very act of willing these they will the universal in the light of the universal, and their activity is consciously aimed at none but the universal end. (pp. 82a-83a)

If there were only subjective freedom, then state and freedom would be opposed, since the state limits the extent to which an individual can do as he pleases. But since there is also objective freedom, the freedom that comes from doing one's duty, the state serves freedom. A subject's duties and rights are determined for him by the state. Hence, in the state, and only in the state, can man be free.

Why is it only in the state that duties and rights are determined? Because, according to Hegel, right is "an existent of any sort embodying the free will" (p. 19a). Right is therefore the concretization or embodiment of freedom, and the state, as the system of rights, is the concretization or embodiment of all freedom.

In Hegel's view of the state, then, there is no opposition between the individual's rights and freedoms on the one side, and the state's rights and demands on the other. There is no need, therefore, for any provisions to safeguard the individual against the encroachments of the state. Such things as Bills of Rights are absurd. The state, not the individual, is supreme. Hegel expresses his idea of the state's grandeur very plainly: "The march of God on earth, that is what the state is" (p. 141a).

III

What is the relation of religion to the state?

This question affords us a good opportunity to see how consistently Hegel applies his principles. In modern times, the separation of church and state has become a cardinal principle of political life in the United States. What is behind this demand for separation? It is based on the view that state and religion are concerned with two different spheres of the individual's life. The state deals with secular matters—with such things as individuals' relations to one another, their property, and their security; religion deals with matters that concern an individual's relation to God—with such things as sin, salvation, and the observance of religious ritual. Since the secular and the religious realms are distinct and both are important, each must respect, and not interfere with, the other.

But, for Hegel, there cannot be any rights that the individual has apart from what the state grants him. This holds true of religion. Religion and religious sentiment are expressions of the person's individuality; they belong to his subjectivity. Now subjectivity has its place in the state; Hegel acknowledges that it is there and that it must be there. Yet the ultimate destiny of subjectivity is always to be transformed and raised up into objectivity. False religion may be opposed to the state and may encourage in the individual ideas that are opposed to the state, that is, thoughts of subjectivity and negativity. On the contrary, however,

if religion be religion of a genuine kind, it does not run counter to the state in a negative or polemical way. . . It rather recognizes the state and upholds it. . . (p. 86c)

And it is to the state's interest that there be such a genuine religion.

The state discharges a duty by affording every assistance and protection to the church in the furtherance of its religious ends; and, in addition, since religion is an integrating factor in the state, implanting a sense of unity in the depths of men's minds, the state should even require all its citizens to belong to a church—*a* church is all that can be said, because since the content of a man's faith depends on his private ideas, the state cannot interfere with it. (p. 86c-d)

The proper relation between church and state, as Hegel sees it, demands that both church and state understand their purpose and essence. Church and religion deal with man's inwardness, his subjectivity. It is wrong for the church to lay claim to the whole realm of truth, as it often does, for this belongs also to the state. The state, on the other hand, being objective rationality, must understand its own supremacy and divine role; it must not deceive itself into thinking that it merely exists as an instrument for the protection and promotion of individuals' rights.

What are the three powers of the state?

Hegel's enumeration differs from the usual one. He begins with the legislature and the executive, but his third power is not the judiciary but rather the "crown." The legislature, in his words, is "the power to determine and establish the universal"; the executive subsumes individual cases under the universal (p. 90c). His definition of the power of the crown is interesting. It is:

the power of subjectivity, as the will with the power of ultimate decision. . . In the crown, the different powers are bound into an individual unity which is thus at once the apex and basis of the whole, i.e. of constitutional monarchy. (p. 90c)

What has become of the judiciary power, in Hegel's system? On p. 97a, he tells us that the "task of merely subsuming the particular under the universal is comprised in the executive power, which also includes the powers of the judiciary and the police."

Is there any great significance in the difference between Hegel's enumeration of the governmental powers and Montesquieu's? Are there really four distinct powers—legislative, executive, judicial, and the crown? What exactly are the functions of the crown? How is it that Montesquieu, whose theoretical discussions drew upon the example of England's constitutional monarchy, did not list the crown as a power?

Is Hegel's view of the powers connected with his over-all view of the state? Does the subsumption of the judiciary under the executive power have any effect on individual liberty?

What are the divisions of the Philosophy of Right?

The divisions arise directly from the method by which the subject of right is treated. This method, Hegel tells us, is that of *dialectic*. The dialectical method takes an idea and considers it in its development. Here, of course, we must first realize that it is an important tenet of Hegel's philosophy that an idea has a development. Ideas are not static things for him; nor are they mere things of the mind. They are, instead, very real and often are embodied in concrete actualities. Ideas are, of course, rational and the development of an idea is

the proper activity of its rationality, and thinking, as something subjective, merely looks on at it without for its part adding to it any ingredient of its own. To consider a thing rationally means not to bring reason to bear on the object from the outside and so to tamper with it, but to find that the object is rational on its own account; here it is mind in its freedom, the culmination of self-conscious reason, which gives itself actuality and engenders itself as an existing world. The sole task of philosophic science is to bring into consciousness this proper work of the reason of the thing itself. (pp. 19d-20a)

The divisions of the *Philosophy of Right*, therefore, correspond to the stages of development of the idea of right. Thus we read:

In correspondence with the stages in the development of the Idea of the absolutely free will, the will is

A. immediate. . .—the sphere of *Abstract* or *Formal Right*;

B. reflected from its external embodiment into itself—it is then characterized as subjective individuality in opposition to the universal . . .—the sphere of *Morality*;

C. the unity and truth of both these abstract moments. . .—*Ethical Life*. (p. 20b-c)

Finally, we need add only that the third division—"Ethical Life"—is again divided into three parts. For "Ethical Life" concerns itself with *first*, the family; *secondly*, civil society; and *thirdly*, the state. The section of the book dealing with the state is again divided into three parts, for the state is first treated in itself, then in relation to other states, and finally insofar as it is a phase of world history.

The *State* [is] freedom, freedom universal and objective even in the free self-subsistence of the particular will. This actual and organic mind (α) of a single nation (β) reveals and actualizes itself through the interrelation of the particular national minds until (γ) in the process of world-history it reveals and actualizes itself as the universal world-mind whose right is supreme. (p. 20c)

The following questions are designed to help you test the thoroughness of your reading. Each question can be answered by giving a page or pages from the reading assignment. Answers will be found on page 221 of this Reading Plan.

1   What is patriotism?

2   Does Hegel think there was a historical social contract?

3   What is Hegel's criticism of Kant's definition of right?

4   Should the state tolerate conscientious objectors?

5   What is the argument against universal suffrage?

6   What is the relation of right and duty?

7   Is war an unqualified evil?

8   What does Hegel think of a "League of Nations" or similar supranational assemblies?

J. S. MILL

On Liberty

Vol. 43, pp. 267–323

T he line between matters that are affected with the public interest and the private concerns of individual men is a difficult one to draw. What part of anyone's life or conduct is nobody else's business, and what part is everybody's business because it affects the lives of others and the welfare of society as a whole? There may be no entirely satisfactory answer to this question, but some determination of what is private and what is public is necessary to determine the proper scope of government and the sphere of individual liberty.

This is the problem John Stuart Mill undertakes to solve in his essay *On Liberty*. We may disagree with where he draws the line between conduct that affects others, or society as a whole, and conduct that affects the individual's private life, but we cannot dismiss the problem as unreal or academic. We need only recall the concrete, practical shape the problem took in the United States during the prohibition era, when there was such an intense difference of opinion about the soundness of the Volstead Act which prohibited the sale of intoxicating liquors. Though it may seem strange to some of us, there was, at an earlier period, a similar conflict about the right of the government to institute compulsory schooling for all children.

In limiting the sphere of government to matters that are affected with the public interest, Mill thinks that individuals are granted as much liberty as they are entitled to and as much as they can safely be allowed. Even though they do not thereby have complete freedom to do whatever they please, they have enough for each man to follow his own bent and lead his own life.

The result is a society which is enriched by the widest variety of individual differences and which, in Mill's view, is at once the free and the good society. Every tendency toward conformity and regimentation, he thinks, is a step in the opposite direction. We cannot read Mill's essay without being compelled to ask whether our society in the twentieth century is moving toward or away from the ideal that he sets before us.

Fifteenth Reading

I

In the guide to the Thirteenth Reading, we have given considerable background material about Mill's life and times. Here it is necessary to add only a few words concerning the essay which constitutes our present reading assignment. Though a short work, it is important. Mill thought highly of it himself. "None of my writings," he says in the *Autobiography* (New York, 1948),

have been either so carefully composed, or so sedulously corrected as this. After it had been written as usual twice over, we kept it by us, bringing it out from time to time, and going through it *de novo*, reading, weighing, and criticizing every sentence. (p. 170)

His wife's death prevented a final, co-operative revision from being made.

The "Liberty" was more directly and literally our joint production than anything else which bears my name, for there was not a sentence of it that was not several times gone through by us together, turned over in many ways, and carefully weeded of any faults, either in thought or expression, that we detected in it. It is in consequence of this that, although it never underwent her final revision, it far surpasses, as a mere specimen of composition, anything which has proceeded from me either before or since. With regard to the thoughts, it is difficult to identify any particular part or element as being more hers than all the rest. The whole mode of thinking of which the book was the expression, was emphatically hers. (pp. 176-177)

Mill felt this essay would be his most lasting work.

The "Liberty" is likely to survive longer than anything else that I have written (with the possible exception of the "Logic"), because the conjunction of her mind with mine has rendered it a kind of philosophic text-book of a single truth, which the changes progressively taking place in modern society tend to bring out into ever stronger relief: the importance, to man and society, of a large variety in types of character, and

209

of giving full freedom to human nature to expand itself in innumerable and conflicting directions. (p. 177)

II

It is strange that in an essay entitled "On Liberty"—an essay, furthermore, which may justly be called a hymn in praise of liberty—we find very little attention paid to the meaning of the term "liberty." Indeed, the only statement that resembles a definition of liberty occurs near the end of the work, and there we find it written very casually: "Liberty consists in doing what one desires" (p. 313b).

But it is from a statement made in the essay's introductory chapter that we get an indication of Mill's point of view.

The only freedom which deserves the name, is that of pursuing our own good in our own way, so long as we do not attempt to deprive others of theirs, or impede their efforts to obtain it. (p. 273a-b)

Here we find two notes that are often repeated in the book. (1) *Positively*, freedom means that a person's individuality is unrestrained. He can do as he pleases; he can pursue his own good; he can pursue it in the way in which he chooses; he can think and express himself as he wishes. (2) *Negatively*, there is but one restriction on this freedom. The exercise of one person's freedom must not interfere with a similar freedom on the part of others. If a man in the free exercise of his individual desires and inclinations harms or threatens to harm other men, or the society in which he and they live, then he may legitimately be restrained and his freedom limited.

Interference by society with a man's freedom is, therefore, warranted only on special occasions. In Mill's opinion these occasions should be rare. In reality, however, society often interferes with men's freedom—much more often than is justified. *On Liberty* is Mill's expression of his belief that society should interfere very little with the individual's freedom. "The object of this Essay," he writes, "is to assert one very simple principle, . . ." and then continues, a little later

That principle is, that the sole end for which mankind are warranted, individually or collectively, in interfering with the liberty of action of any of their number, is self-protection. (p. 271c-d)

The essay deals with both the positive and negative aspect of freedom. Chapters 2 and 3 indicate the reasons why freedom is a basic human good. Chapter 2 shows that freedom of thought and discussion is desirable; Chapter 3 attempts to demonstrate that freedom in the sense of seeking one's own good in one's own way is highly desirable. Chapter 4 then turns to the negative side of the problem, namely, the extent to which society is justified in interfering with the individual's freedom. These three chapters constitute the main body of the work; they are surrounded by Chapters 1 and 5 which are introductory and concluding in character.

III

The full title of Chapter 3 is "Of Individuality, as one of the Elements of Well-being." Having shown in the previous chapter that the expression of opinions should be free, Mill now wishes to inquire

whether the same reasons do not require that men should be free to act upon their opinions—to carry these out in their lives, without hindrance, either physical or moral, from their fellow-men, so long as it is at their own risk and peril. (p. 293b-c)

If Mill can succeed in showing that the free development of individuality is a human end, that is, that it is part of happiness, there will be little difficulty in persuading men that the proper means to this end is to permit the greatest possible freedom of action. The difficult task is not to show that freedom is needed for individuality, but rather that individuality is in itself something desirable. Most men, Mill tells us over and over again in this chapter, do not think so.

If it were felt that the free development of individuality is one of the leading essentials of well-being; that it is not only a coordinate element with all that is designated by the terms civilisation, instruction, education, culture, but is itself a necessary part and condition of all those things; there would be no danger that liberty should be undervalued, and the adjustment of the boundaries between it and social control would present no extraordinary difficulty. (p. 294a)

But in fact there is no such appreciation of individuality.

Individual spontaneity is hardly recognised by the common modes of thinking as having any intrinsic worth, or deserving any regard on its own account. The majority, being satisfied with the ways of mankind as they now are . . . cannot comprehend why those ways should not be good enough for everybody. . . (*Ibid.*)

The rest of this chapter is, therefore, a continuing lament about the low esteem in which individuality is held, together with an assortment of reasons why it *should* be highly regarded.

Why is it to a person's advantage to be able to give full vent to his individuality, his originality, his own desires and impulses? The answer is obvious. No one maintains that men should all be copies of one another; nor could they be, even if they tried. To be sure, men should learn from the experiences of others, but there is a definite limit to how far this can be carried. The experience of others is suitable for their circumstances and conditions; it may not be suitable for us. Nor can a man rely on customs, for

customs are made for customary circumstances and customary characters; and his circumstances or his character may be uncustomary. (p. 294d)

However, according to Mill, there is another and more important reason. Only by acting for himself and choosing for himself can a man develop in himself "any of the qualities which are the distinctive endowment of a human being." These are qualities such as the faculties of perception, judgment, discrimination, and, in general, mental activity. All these powers require exercise in order to flourish. "The mental and moral, like the muscular powers, are improved only by being used." No doubt, men will make mistakes in using these powers. But they will learn from their mistakes and such experience will make them more valuable persons. The full development of the human being is, perhaps, the supreme end for Mill. For the sake of this development he would be willing to put up with many mistakes and many inconveniences.

Supposing it were possible to get houses built, corn grown, battles fought, causes tried, and even churches erected and prayers said, by machinery —by automatons in human form—it would be a considerable loss to exchange for these automatons even the men and women who at present

MILL: *On Liberty* 213

inhabit the more civilised parts of the world, and who assuredly are but starved specimens of what nature can and will produce. (p. 295b)

The full development of the human person goes beyond mental powers. The individual's desires and impulses must likewise be permitted to develop freely and to be a person's own. Mankind will be even less likely to concede the worth of fully developed desires than of intellectual powers, Mill realizes, but he has powerful arguments to support his view.

A person whose desires and impulses are his own—are the expression of his own nature, as it has been developed and modified by his own culture—is said to have a character. One whose desires and impulses are not his own, has no character, no more than a steam-engine has a character. (p. 295d)

Mill complains, in 1859, that men do not appreciate the values of individuality. They may pay lip service to them, but in the majority of cases they prefer the uniformity and customariness of routine lives.

Not only in what concerns others, but in what concerns only themselves, the individual or the family do not ask themselves—what do I prefer? or, what would suit my character and disposition? or, what would allow the best and highest in me to have fair play, and enable it to grow and thrive? They ask themselves, what is suitable to my position? what is usually done by persons of my station and pecuniary circumstances? or (worse still) what is usually done by persons of a station and circumstances superior to mine? I do not mean that they choose what is customary in preference to what suits their own inclination. It does not occur to them to have any inclination, except for what is customary. (p. 296a-b)

Today we are complaining about the same things that bothered Mill one hundred years ago. We decry the uniformity of tastes, of desires, and actions. We find depressing sameness in the houses people live in; in the entertainments they watch; in the cars they drive; and, worst of all, in the thoughts they have. We are accustomed to attributing much of this to our mass culture, that is, to mass production of goods, to mass mediums of communication such as television, to the fact that a few magazines and newspapers with huge circulations blanket the nation. All these things tend to concentrate the determination of what our life shall be like in the hands of a few, instead of in each individual person's desires and opinions. This process of making everybody uniform had already begun in Mill's time:

> Comparatively speaking, [all men] now read the same things, listen to the same things, see the same things, go to the same places, have their hopes and fears directed to the same objects, have the same rights and liberties, and the same means of asserting them. Great as are the differences of position which remain, they are nothing to those which have ceased. And the assimilation is still proceeding. All the political changes of the age promote it. . . Every extension of education promotes it. . . Improvement in the means of communication promotes it . . . The increase of commerce and manufactures promotes it. . . A more powerful agency than even all these, in bringing about a general similarity among mankind, is the complete establishment, in this and other free countries, of the ascendancy of public opinion in the State. (p. 302a-b)

These factors that endanger individuality increase Mill's vigor in arguing for its values. When he speaks of individuality, he does not have in mind merely a genteel oddness; he really means to encourage unusual behavior and thought. As unequivocally as possible, Mill proclaims the virtues of "eggheads," bohemians, and other rebels against established society.

> Precisely because the tyranny of opinion is such as to make eccentricity a reproach, it is desirable, in order to break through that tyranny, that people should be eccentric. Eccentricity has always abounded when and where strength of character has abounded; and the amount of eccentricity in a society has generally been proportional to the amount of genius, mental vigour, and moral courage it contained. That so few now dare to be eccentric marks the chief danger of the time. (p. 299a)

IV

What are Mill's arguments in favor of liberty of thought and discussion?

Every man's opinions, whether right or wrong, ought to be permitted to be expressed, discussed, and disseminated, Mill tells us.

> If the opinion is right, [men] are deprived of the opportunity of exchanging error for truth: if wrong, they lose, what is almost as great a benefit, the clearer perception and livelier impression of truth, produced by its collision with error. (p. 275a)

In this view, should free discussion of *any* opinion put forth (in public discussion, in the newspapers, etc.) be permitted? Or are there any opinions the suppression of which Mill would think justified?

Suppose an opinion exists which is known to be true—as much as this ever can be known. Must an opinion contradictory to it still be permitted to circulate? What purpose can it serve to give full public hearing to error? Does Mill's view not lead to the result that men will never learn from their ancestors' experience? Why must every generation repeat the errors of previous ones?

Does the freedom of opinion which Mill advocates extend to all subjects? Or are any excepted? For instance, are theological matters to be excepted in a country—like England— where there is an established church? Would Mill be likely to advocate freedom of opinion in the field of mathematics? Is the opinion that "$5 + 2 = 8$" to be tolerated? Must it be permitted to exist in the classroom?

At the beginning of Chapter 2, Mill tells us that one reason for advocating freedom of thought and discussion *used* to be that it constituted a powerful defense against the establishment of tyrannical governments. But now—meaning in 1858—this argument is granted on all sides, and freedom of thought is suppressed in other ways and for other reasons. Mill, therefore, pays no further attention to the role of freedom of thought and expression in subduing the tyrannical ambitions of men. But we may consider the matter here for a moment.

Does the press in the United States nowadays function, at least in part, to protect the republican form of government? What is the difference between publishing "exposés" for the sake of building circulation and for the sake of serving the public?

The president of the United States holds news conferences at regular intervals. This is not prescribed in the Constitution, nor by any law. Do these conferences contribute to the spirit of liberty in the United States? Or are they just silly exhibitions of reporters trying to catch the president in errors? Is the exposure of the president's opinions to close questioning compatible with the dignity of his office?

It is sometimes said that "the public business must be public," that is, that there must be no closed sessions of legislatures, city councils, etc. Would these bodies sometimes not function more efficiently and more courageously if their deliberations were not subject to public scrutiny? Is the loss in efficiency made up for by a gain in liberty?

Are there any restrictions on freedom of action?

There are more strictures on this kind of freedom than on that of thought and discussion, because actions often involve other men. Of course, opinions—if propagated—also may involve other men and then they, too, are subject to some restrictions.

An opinion that corn-dealers are starvers of the poor, or that private property is robbery, ought to be unmolested when simply circulated through the press, but may justly incur punishment when delivered orally to an excited mob assembled before the house of a corn-dealer, or when handed about among the same mob in the form of a placard. (p. 293c)

And so it is even more true that actions cease to be permissible when they harm or threaten to harm other men. "Acts, of whatever kind, which, without justifiable cause, do harm to others, may be, and in the more important cases absolutely require to be, controlled by the unfavourable sentiments, and, when needful, by the active interference of mankind" (p. 293c). In Chapter 4, Mill sums up his view of the relation of society and individual in these words:

As soon as any part of a person's conduct affects prejudicially the interests of others, society has jurisdiction over it, and the question whether the general welfare will or will not be promoted by interfering with it, becomes open to discussion. But there is no room for entertaining any such question when a person's conduct affects the interests of no persons besides himself, or needs not affect them unless they like. . . (p. 303a)

Is the distinction between an individual's acts that affect only himself and acts that affect other members of society a tenable one? Are there ever any acts, besides that of thinking, which do not in some way affect other men? And are these men and society therefore justified in interfering with these acts? In other words, does Mill's doctrine leave any room for freedom of action? Could not Mill's theory that a man's acts may be interfered with by society if they affect society lead to a high degree of state regulation? Does Mill face this question? If he does, what is his answer to it?

In Mill's opinion, can a properly made law interfere with freedom? For instance, would he have thought that the eighteenth amendment to the Constitution of the United States was inimical to freedom?

Is it Mill's view that it is the purpose of laws to make men virtuous? In this, does he agree with Thomas Aquinas? Does Mill think that laws should ever protect men from doing harm to themselves?

The following questions are designed to help you test the thoroughness of your reading. Each question is to be answered by giving a page or pages of the reading assignment. Answers will be found on page 221 of this Reading Plan.

1 How does the career of Emperor Marcus Aurelius illustrate the need for freedom of thought and discussion?

2 How does Mill justify despotism as a form of government for some peoples?

3 How does Mill describe the Calvinistic doctrine of human nature?

4 What are the two conditions of human development which Mill advocates, following Von Humboldt?

5 What are Mill's opinions concerning legislation to protect the Sabbath?

6 Is it legitimate to tax liquor at a high rate in order to discourage its use?

7 Should marriages be prevented by the state if there appears to be insufficient money to bring up and educate any possible offspring?

ANSWERS

First Reading

1. 347a–d
2. 346c–347a
3. 352d–353a
4. 311c–312b
5. 316b–318c, esp. 318b
6. 321a–324a
7. 342a–c
8. 344a–c
9. 341c–d
10. 367b–c

Second Reading

1. 472a–b
2. 475d, 488a
3. 477a–c
4. 481a–b
5. 482a–c
6. 489b–d
7. 491a–492a
8. 493c
9. 493d

Third Reading

1. 651c
2. 652c
3. 653b–c
4. 657a
5. 661b–d
6. 668c–d
7. 675d–677a
8. 678b–d
9. 683a–b
10. 683b–c
11. 686a–b
12. 688a–c

Fourth Reading

1. I Samuel 14:24–46,
   (D) I Kings 14:24–46
2. Acts 23:8
3. Acts 22:3
4. I Samuel 15,
   (D) I Kings 15
5. Acts 24:1–9
6. I Samuel 18:5–9,
   (D) I Kings 18:5–9
7. I Samuel 16:23,
   (D) I Kings 16:23
8. I Samuel 31:1–6,
   (D) I Kings 31:1–6

Fifth Reading

1. 168b
2. 133b
3. 12d
4. 130a–b
5. 141c–143c
6. 156a–b
7. 169a–b
8. 172c–173c

Sixth Reading

1. 214d–215a, c
2. 224c–d
3. 229d–230a
4. 233a–d
5. 219c
6. 214a–b
7. 227b–c
8. 234d
9. 234b–c

Seventh Reading

1. 18a–c
2. 32a–d
3. 14a–c
4. 22a
5. 24c–d
6. 8a–c
7. 25a–d
8. 33d–34b
9. 23d–24d

Eighth Reading

1. 112d–113a
2. 94b–c
3. 93b
4. 113b–c
5. 102c–103a
6. 96a–b
7. 105a
8. 115a–116b
9. 86c–d
10. 85d–86a

Ninth Reading

1. 483a
2. 438a–439a
3. 453d–454a
4. 462a–b
5. 465c
6. 487b
7. 491a–b
8. 496b–c

Tenth Reading

1. 57a–b
2. 61b, d–62a
3. 5c
4. 6a
5. 38d–39c
6. 71b–c
7. 99b–c
8. 15d–16a

Eleventh Reading

1. 388b–c
2. 391a–b
3. 397d–398a
4. 405a–c
5. 394d
6. 389c–d
7. 393c–d
8. 406a–d

Twelfth Reading

1. 437c–d, 450d–451a
2. 450b
3. 399b–400a
4. 439a–441b
5. 438a–439a
6. 449d
7. 449c
8. 445c–446a

Thirteenth Reading

1. 333c–334c
2. 341d–344c
3. 345b–c
4. 388c–389a
5. 356c–d
6. 359a–361b
7. 383b–d
8. 346c–348b

Fourteenth Reading

1. 84c–d
2. 80d–81a
3. 19a–b
4. 86d–87b (fn. 1)
5. 104a
6. 83b–d
7. 107a–d
8. 109b–c

Fifteenth Reading

1. 279a–d
2. 272a–b
3. 296b–d
4. 294b, 302a–d
5. 310c–311a
6. 315c-d
7. 319b–d

ADDITIONAL READINGS

1. By the authors of *Great Books of the Western World*

THUCYDIDES, *The History of the Peloponnesian War*

PLATO, *The Republic,* Books VIII-IX; *Statesman; Laws*

ARISTOTLE, *Politics,* Books V-VIII

PLUTARCH, "Alcibiades," "Coriolanus," "Demosthenes," "Cicero," in *The Lives of the Noble Grecians and Romans*

TACITUS, *The Histories*

THOMAS AQUINAS, *On the Governance of Rulers,* rev. ed. London: Sheed and Ward, 1938

DANTE, *De Monarchia* or *On World-Government.* New York: Liberal Arts Press, 1949

MACHIAVELLI, *Discourses.* New York: The Modern Library, 1940

HOBBES, *Leviathian,* Ch. 22-31

SHAKESPEARE, *Julius Caesar; Coriolanus*

SPINOZA, B. "Political Treatise." In *The Chief Works of Spinoza,* 3d ed., 2 vol. New York: Dover Publications, 1952 "Theologico-Political Treatise." *Ibid.*

LOCKE, "First Treatise of Government." In *Two Treatises of Government.* New York: Hafner Publishing Co., 1940.

MONTESQUIEU, *The Spirit of Laws,* Books XIV-XXXI *Considerations on the Causes of the Grandeur and Decadence of the Romans.* New York: D. Appleton and Co., 1912

ROUSSEAU, *The Social Contract,* Books III-IV; *A Discourse on the Origin of Inequality*

KANT, *Perpetual Peace.* New York: Columbia University Press, 1939

J. S. MILL, *Autobiography.* New York: Columbia University Press, 1944 *The Subjection of Women.* New York: E. P. Dutton and Co., 1929

HEGEL, *Philosophy of History,* Introduction

2. By other authors

Basic Ideas of Alexander Hamilton, ed. by Richard B. Morris. New York: The Pocket Library, 1957

BOSANQUET, BERNARD, *The Philosophical Theory of the State.* London: Macmillan and Co., Ltd., 1950

BRITTON, KARL, *John Stuart Mill.* Pelican Series

BURKE, EDMUND, "An Appeal from the New to the Old Whigs." In *The Works of the Right Honorable Edmund Burke.* London: World's Classics, Oxford University Press "Reflections on the Revolution in France." *Ibid.*

CALHOUN, JOHN, "A Disquisition on Government." In *Basic Documents.* State College, Pa.: Bald Eagle Press, 1952

CASSIRER, ERNST, *The Myth of the State.* New Haven: Yale University Press, 1946 *The Question of Jean-Jacques Rousseau.* New York: Columbia University Press, 1954

CHAFEE, ZECHARIAH, JR., *The Blessings of Liberty.* New York: J. B. Lippincott Co., 1954

CORWIN, EDWARD S., *Liberty Against Government.* Baton Rouge: Louisiana State University Press, 1948

CRANSTON, MAURICE W., *John Locke, a Biography.* New York: The Macmillan Company, 1957

CROCE, BENEDETTO, *Politics and Morals.* London: George Allen and Unwin, Ltd., 1946

GILBY, THOMAS, *The Political Thought of Thomas Aquinas.* Chicago: The University of Chicago Press, 1958

GOUGH, J. W., *John Locke's Political Philosophy.* London: Oxford University Press, 1950

GREEN, T. H., *The Principles of Political Obligation,* 2d ed. New York: Longmans, Green and Co., 1942

HALE, ROBERT L., *Freedom Through Law.* New York: Columbia University Press, 1952

HOBHOUSE, T. L., *Liberalism.* London: Home University Library, Oxford University Press, 1944 *The Metaphysical Theory of the State.* London: George Allen and Unwin, Ltd., 1951

JOUVENAL, BERTRAND DE, *Sovereignty.* Chicago: The University of Chicago Press, 1957

KELSEN, HANS, *General Theory of Law and the State*. Cambridge: Harvard University Press, 1949

KIRK, RUSSELL A., *The Conservative Mind from Burke to Santayana*. Chicago: Henry Regnery Co., 1953

LASKI, HAROLD, J., *A Grammar of Politics*, 2nd ed. New Haven: Yale University Press, 1931
Liberty in the Modern State. Harmondsworth, Middlesex, Eng.: Penguin Books, 1937
The State in Theory and Practice. New York: The Viking Press, 1935

LENIN, NIKOLAI, *The State and Revolution*. Moscow: Foreign Languages Publishing House, 1949

LINDSAY, ALEXANDER D., *The Modern Democratic State*. London: Oxford University Press, 1947

LIPPMANN, WALTER, *Essays in the Public Philosophy*. Boston: Little, Brown and Co., 1955

MacIVER, ROBERT, *The Web of Government*. New York: The Macmillan Company, 1947

MARITAIN, JACQUES, *Scholasticism and Politics*, 2d ed. New York: The Macmillan Company, 1952

MILL, JAMES, "An Essay on Government." In *The English Philosophers from Bacon to Mill*, ed. by E. A. Burtt. New York: The Modern Library, 1939

MILLSPAUGH, ARTHUR C., *Democracy, Efficiency, Stability*. Washington, D.C.: The Brookings Institution, 1942

NEUMANN, FRANZ L., *The Democratic and the Authoritarian State*. Chicago, Ill.: The Free Press, 1957

NICHOLS, JEANNETTE P., AND NICHOLS, ROY F., *The Growth of American Democracy*. New York: D. Appleton-Century, Inc., 1939

O'CONNER, D. J., *Locke*. Ch. IX, Pelican Series, 1952

PACKE, MICHAEL ST. JOHN, *The Life of John Stuart Mill*. London: Secker and Warburg, 1954

PAINE, THOMAS, *The Rights of Man*. New York: Everyman's Library, E. P. Dutton and Co., 1916

PARKINSON, C. NORTHCOTE, *The Evolution of Political Thought*. New York: Houghton Mifflin Company, 1958

PETERS, RICHARD, *Hobbes*. Pelican Series

Popper, Karl R., *The Open Society and Its Enemies*. Princeton, N.J.: Princeton University Press, 1950

Selected Writings of John and John Quincy Adams, ed. by A. Kock and W. Peden. New York: Alfred A. Knopf, 1946

Simon, Yves, *Philosophy of Democratic Government*. Chicago: The University of Chicago Press, 1951

Strauss, Leo, *The Political Philosophy of Hobbes*. London: The Oxford Press, 1936

Tocqueville, Alexis de, *Democracy in America*. New York: Alfred A. Knopf, Inc., 1952

Warrender, Howard, *The Political Philosophy of Hobbes*. London: The Oxford Press, 1957

Wild, John D., *Plato's Modern Enemies and the Theory of Natural Law*. Chicago: The University of Chicago Press, 1953